Wellington, N.Z.

EQUATOR

shington
Ottawa

I

PACIFIC OCEAN

NORTH
POLE
+

London

IV

VIII

Berlin

Moscow

II

Tokyo

Peking

III

New Delhi

VI

VII

XI
Canberra

Singapore

INDIAN OCEAN

D1202027

World Power Assessment 1977

World Power Assessment 1977

A CALCULUS OF STRATEGIC DRIFT

RAY S. CLINE

WESTVIEW PRESS
BOULDER, COLORADO

Published in cooperation with

THE CENTER FOR
STRATEGIC AND
INTERNATIONAL STUDIES
WASHINGTON, D.C.

Copyright © 1977 by Ray S. Cline

Published in 1977 in the United States of America by
  Westview Press, Inc.
  1898 Flatiron Court
  Boulder, Colorado 80301
  Frederick A. Praeger, Publisher and Editorial Director
Library of Congress Card Number: 77-10198
ISBN: 0-89158-237-1

Printed and bound in the United States of America

Contents

MAPS, CHARTS, AND GRAPHS

Foreword

There are many assessments of the military balance—both nuclear and conventional—within the framework of world power relationships, but most have a largely quantitative and technical focus. What has been lacking is an overall conceptual methodology that incorporates these military factors with the broader geopolitical, economic, and psychological issues that tend to determine the outcome of real international conflicts. It is this need that Dr. Ray S. Cline undertook to fill with his first *World Power Assessment,* issued in 1975, in which he developed and employed a novel methodology and terminology.

The 1975 version of this book was widely acclaimed and has been put to good use not only by scholars but also by policymakers, the news media, and students. One enthusiastic reviewer went so far as to compare Dr. Cline's formula for measuring perceived power favorably with the somewhat more famous nuclear energy formula, $E = mc^2$.

The Georgetown University Center for Strategic and International Studies (CSIS) is proud to bring out this updated assessment reflecting not only new data but the substance of the many dialogues engendered by Dr. Cline's first volume. This 1977 edition considerably refines and extends some of the concepts of measuring international power in accordance with the concept for which he coined the word "politectonic." It further assesses the trend line indicating the likelihood of future conflict or stability and identifies critical elements that must be taken into account in U.S. strategic thinking and foreign policy as of 1977. We feel that this new study is especially relevant and timely as the United States, under new national leadership, faces the turbulent international environment of the remainder of the 1970s.

DAVID M. ABSHIRE
Chairman, CSIS

Author's Preface

My hope in writing this book is that readers will be stimulated to realistic thinking about world affairs and the necessary ingredients of an effective U.S. foreign policy. Whatever value there is in this assessment of the balance of world power derives from exchanges of ideas and information with all of the friends and associates with whom I worked for many years in the Central Intelligence Agency and the Department of State as well as, more recently, at Georgetown University.

I am deeply appreciative for the sterling assistance given during the preparation of *World Power Assessment 1977* by my able research editor, Sylvia Lowe; by Mary Cobb, who diligently, even heroically, prepared the manuscript for publication; and by my wife, Marjorie W. Cline, who compiled the index with great competence and good humor. Finally, I am grateful to my personal secretarial and research assistants, Ann Campagna and Ona Gelman, for their many contributions to the completion of the whole task of research and writing.

RAY S. CLINE

Washington, D.C.
March 1, 1977

CHAPTER ONE

Politectonics: Measuring the Strength of Nations

T he political and economic structure of international relations has never been more complex and challenging than at this time when a new national political leadership under President James E. Carter is taking hold of the reins of power. Whatever the United States does or refrains from doing abroad materially affects the fate of nations and peoples whose welfare is tied to the fortunes of the strongest country in the world. From the vantage point of Washington the view looks out over a sea of challenges; the question uppermost in most of the capitals of the world is whether the political will and coherence of purpose in the United States is adequate to those challenges, which present great opportunities as well as great dangers.

The low point in American fortunes was reached in 1974 with the removal from office of an incumbent President for the first time in U.S. history. Alliances hitherto thought vital to U.S. security seemed to be drifting apart or simply drifting. In Vietnam the United States suffered the first clearcut military defeat ever inflicted on it. As a result, the world witnessed a humiliating U.S. withdrawal from the Indochina area and the collapse of a regime and a society in which successive U.S. presidents had invested heavily in terms of lives, money, and prestige. The buoyancy of earlier U.S. behavior trailed off into national uncertainty, indecisiveness, and self-doubt. Public confidence in government policymaking reached its lowest point since before World War II.

Since 1975 the country has appeared to be gradually recovering its spirit and vigor. The bicentennial year brought a lift to public spirits and some longer perspective to the public view of the more recent travails of the country. The economy has resumed its growth. A new political leadership has been elected and taken office with a mandate to restore confidence and build a national consensus behind American national purposes at home and abroad. It is more generally realized now than in the past two or three years that, the frustration of U.S. strategic efforts in Vietnam notwithstanding, the United States still has enormous economic and military power which needs only to be focused on the pursuit of a coherent national purpose or strategy on which there is political consensus. The beginning of an upswing in U.S. drive and performance is only now in 1977 registering on the crude scale of international perceptions of power factors. It is crucial to understand what is happening in the international arena that has brought about these changes and to calibrate just where the United States really stands in the scale of world power. This book suggests some answers. They emerge upon looking at the strength of nations in terms of global geography, economic interdependence, military capability, and shifting political alignments.

There is nothing very new in this approach to our problems. It is really a return to basics and the long perspectives of historical change. Shortly after the turn of the twentieth century, in 1904, the great British geographer, Sir Halford Mackinder, wrote an essay on "The Geographical Pivot of History" emphasizing the pivotal significance of political control of the human and material resources of the central Eurasian land mass on the international scene. This emphasis increased as his ideas evolved more precisely down into the period of World War II. As the core of his thinking, Mackinder articulated a crucial concept in international relations by declaring that command of the Eurasian heartland (essentially Central Europe and Russia, from the Rhine to the Urals) would eventually lead to command of all of the world's resources and peoples. The pros and cons of this dictum have formed the core of most informed discussion of strategic theory ever since. Napoleon, Hitler, and Stalin all came very close to seizing control of that heartland. The USSR commands most of this region today. Mackinder looks more prescient every day as we search for insights into present international circumstances.

There is a striking analogy between present political and strategic trends, on the one hand, and the terminology of new scholarly findings relating to the seabeds, as well as fundamental new geological concepts, on the other. It now seems that the earth's surface is made up of a number of separate "tectonic plates"[1] containing entire continents and immense stretches of the surrounding seabeds. There is a North American plate, a South American plate, a Pacific plate, a China plate, a Eurasian plate, an African plate, and an Indian Ocean-Australian plate as well as some smaller regional pieces of the earth's outer crustal shell. These continental plates float on a more fluid inner core, and they have very slowly drifted apart and then together over the millennia. Where they meet or pull apart, mountain ranges are thrust up, volcanic and seismic pressures erupt, the great oceanic ridges and rifts are formed, and some underwater terrain slips beneath the edge of adjoining tectonic plates and is slowly ground down back into the molten core of the earth.

A more graphic picture of what is taking place in a much quicker time frame in the shifting of international power in this century could hardly be found. The strength of nations and of the clusters of nations allied to one another waxes and wanes in conformity with subterranean rhythms of economic, military, and political currents producing either growth and stability or conflict, erosion, and destruction.

No good word is in common use to describe the process of analyzing such structural international changes. The old term, "geopolitics," which derives from Mackinder's model for world trends, fell into disrepute some time ago, largely as a result of distortions introduced in Germany by Karl Haushofer in Hitler's time. In its place we now most often hear theorists talk of a geometric—triangular, pentagonal, etc.— "balance of power" vaguely reminiscent of Metternichean Europe. This talk has proved to be largely irrelevant to what is actually taking place in the twentieth century. The economics and ideology of the nineteenth century "concert of Europe" among nations very similar in political structure are not very helpful in explaining the relations between the pluralistic U.S. open society and the autarchic dictatorships of the Soviet Union or the People's Republic of China (PRC). The structure of international ties and conflicts is based on politics and geography, not geometry. A more realistic model is needed for analyzing today's power distribution among nations.

Accordingly, this book undertakes to study the elements of power in international politics and the gradual shift in the balance of those elements among nations and groups of nations in terms of a new formula based on old truths. To suggest the geographical foundations of this method of strategic analysis, and yet emphasize that the kind of power we are talking about is essentially political, economic, and military, I have used a new word, "politectonics," i.e., political structuring. By this, I mean to denote the formation and breakup of international power groupings, mainly regional in makeup, but also shaped by cultural, political, and economic forces, that determine the real balance in today's give-and-take relations among nations.

In keeping with this approach, this analysis is centered on the United States, the foremost single continent-sized unit of national power, and on the clusters of nations which associate themselves in one or more ways, some closely, some loosely, with the power of the United States. In addition, we analyze those clusters of nations which stand apart from the United States and, in some cases, directly or indirectly oppose U.S. power and influence.

By this method, we describe the world as made up of a number of discrete politectonic zones. The future international alignments of major nations within these are crucial. There are eleven such zones, as shown on the frontispiece map, of which the primary ones are: (I) North America, the heartland of which is the United States; (II) the USSR, the heartland of Eurasia; and (III) China (PRC) and the Asian Communist regimes in Korea and Indochina, which together occupy most of the mainland of East Asia.

On the periphery of Eurasia are five great peninsular or insular zones, the rimlands, which can be dominated from the center of the continental land mass but which are also at this time in history closely connected by transoceanic ties to other parts of the world. These five are: (IV) West Europe, the crucial, long-disputed area stretching from Greece to the United Kingdom, an extended Eurasian peninsula from the viewpoint of the Soviet heartland; (V) the Mideast, a long, disorganized belt of nations reaching from Iran across Asia Minor and the Arabian peninsula to the Arab littoral of North Africa; (VI) South Asia, the subcontinent; (VII) Southeast Asia beyond Indochina, the vast ocean archipelago area containing Indonesia, the Philippines, Singapore, Malaysia, Thailand, and Burma; and (VIII) Northeast Asia, the Japan—South Korea—China/Taiwan triangle.

These zones, the rimlands of Eurasia, are surrounded by an outer circle of continents and peoples. This circle comprises mainly the lands of the southern hemisphere, which group themselves in three zones: (IX) South America; (X) Central and Southern Africa, and (XI) Australia and New Zealand.

Needless to say, other dividing lines between zones could be picked out and there are several geographical regions, like the Caribbean or the Arabian and Iranian geological plates, that can be viewed as separate politectonic subzones. The eleven basic zones, however, provide a useful structural overview of international relations today. The power of the individual nations in each zone and their links with one another as well as their relationships with nations in other zones are the stuff with which world strategy and diplomacy deal. The slow, sometimes nearly imperceptible shifting and drifting of the dominant elements in these zones, the dynamics of clusters of allied nations, whether they are tightly controlled empires or voluntary associations of countries, are what we are observing.

This gradual movement within and back and forth among zones is indeed like the drift of continental plates on the earth's surface. The insights gained through this politectonic approach to international power largely coincide with the conventional wisdom of most Americans about international power and conflict in recent years. Attempts to measure the power of nations individually or in groups are exceedingly difficult and inexact, whatever approach is used. Judging the trend in power relationships among the earth's politectonic zones is even more difficult. Looking at the United States' place in today's power structure from such a viewpoint may, however, clarify an understanding of the dangers and opportunities in the world around us in an era of strategic drift.

Nations

In the rhetorical atmosphere of the United Nations all of the 158 more or less sovereign nations[2] of the world are equal, but everyone is aware that in the real world some nations are much "more equal" than others. Some have tremendous power, others very little. In modern times the nation-state is the main aggregative unit of political force in international affairs.

A nation is a group of people, usually living in a specific territory, who share a common sense of history, customs, and—usually—language. A state is a sovereign body politic. Many modern states are homogeneous nations and many nations are sovereign states. On the other hand, there are many states which are multinational, as in the USSR, where the dominant Great Russian population constitutes barely more than half of a country which includes many still quite distinct cultural minorities concentrated in specific regions like the Ukraine or Kazakhstan that by any normal definition would make up nations in their own right. The United States is a quite different type of nation-state with an astonishing mix of ethnic groups, many of whom deliberately came to North America to belong to a pluralistic body politic of remarkable political, cultural, and linguistic homogeneity.

Within national boundaries in many parts of the world, especially in Asia and Africa, tribalism or ethnic subnational loyalties are strong. Religious minorities and ethnic or linguistic factions battle in Ireland and Belgium and India, and create agonizing tensions in Cyprus, South Africa, and even in Canada. The melting pot does not always really meld, not even in the United States, as fast or as thoroughly as once supposed. Nevertheless, the nation-state is the decisive political unit of action and responsibility in our era. Decisions in international conflicts or collaborations are made by the political leadership in power at any given time in each of the 158 nations.

From the town meeting to the nation-state, communities of all types and sizes dispense power and privileges insofar as they act as a group. All of them must work out systems for sharing benefits and burdens, as well as for settling disputes among their members. They must also set up some kind of sanctions to enforce compliance with those settlements, sanctions vested in some constituted authority, whether it is an absolute monarch with his army or a judiciary backed by civil police. Ultimately, power is the ability to coerce. Making decisions on all these matters is the business of government.

In a community embracing the whole world, at this period of history, there is no single legitimately constituted power for the effective settlement of disagreements about economic, military, and political conflicts. More important, there is no procedure in international relations which guarantees that sanctions will be applied to enforce compliance with such international settlements as can be agreed upon. The extent to which one country can pursue its international and domestic aims without regard to, or even against, the interests of others, is based in the final analysis on its own national power as compared with that of other nations. Power in the international arena can thus be defined simply as the ability of the government of one state to cause the government of another state to do something which the latter otherwise would not choose to do—whether by persuasion, coercion, or outright military force.

Power is a subjective fact; it need not actually be brought into use to arrive at the results desired by those who wield it. A nation's leaders make decisions affecting foreign policy on the basis of projections of what they perceive their own power to be or of what they think is the power of others. Such projections may not always be accurate; there is often a marked lag between changing facts and perceptions of them, but the perceptions nonetheless determine governmental decisions.

International conflicts of interest, whether political, economic, or military, are played out like games of chess. Perceived power is a decisive factor, even if it only prevents another's action, like a chessman which threatens every square on the board to which an opponent's piece might move. The threat may never be carried out and therefore superficially nothing may appear to have happened. As on a chessboard, however, the pattern of potential power and counter-power in the minds of the antagonists determines how the game proceeds from move to move and how it will end. Sometimes one nation carries out its aims to complete victory. More often the match is indecisive or flatly stalemated. Only in desperate cases does the struggle move into a true end game, when—in international affairs—other levels of political and economic conflict are transcended and nations at last resort to war.

A study of national power, in the final analysis, is a study of the capacity to wage war, but it is also in the normal run of cases an appraisal of many other kinds of international competition or conflict, where differences are resolved within a political or an economic context. It is important to calculate carefully the capabilities and intentions of enemies or potential enemies. Thus, in thinking about an appropriate strategy for the United States and the strategic balance which we seek in the world, it is essential to return to some positive ideas about which nations in the world are sympathetic toward U.S. purposes and which of them are strong enough to be helpful to the United States. It is at this point that moral or political considerations come into play in foreign policy and strategy.

A nation cannot afford to become mesmerized by the power potential of an adversary. An obsessive preoccupation with hostile governments can lead to error, either through exaggerated fear of the dangers they present or through anxiety to placate them. The *sine qua non* is to recognize national objectives and to estimate whether or not they can be achieved. This will depend upon our own national power plus that power committed to our side by dependable alliances. Like good friends, good allies must be shown again and again the mutual benefits of free and voluntary association. As Walter Lippmann said, 30 years ago:

> American commitments and interests and ideals must be covered by our armaments, our strategic frontiers, and our alliances.[3]

These basics—military strength, strategic position, and alliances—are what we must examine in the light of the real international environment today. Circumstances change drastically but the basics persist. The U.S. problem is complicated by the fact that the whole era since World War II is in many ways unique, unprecedented. It has seen a vast explosion of populations and technologies, along with a proliferation of economic goods and services.

For the first time in history two nations greater in most respects than any of the rest, the United States and the Soviet Union, each plainly possess the capability of using nuclear weapons and their delivery systems to destroy the cities and total industrial structure of the other, or of any nation. This fact acts as a restraint on the use of military force by all nations to pursue their national objectives at the expense of others. It also constitutes heavy psychological pressure on weaker nations to conform with the wishes of the two great nuclear powers and, in some cases, acts to prevent conflicts at levels of intensity lower than total warfare. In many cases restraints on resort to terror or small-scale military action are diminishing because of the widespread belief that the nuclear powers will never dare to use their immensely destructive weapons.

Gradually, over the past quarter century, it has become apparent that the ultimate sanction of maximum nuclear destruction is, in fact, if not quite "unthinkable," too awful—in the true sense of that much abused word—to contemplate except as a desperate defensive last resort. Thus it is unlikely to be employed except in those improbable circumstances where such drastic punishment would fit the provocation. Lesser crimes of nation-states tend to be dealt with by the conventional methods of diplomacy, economic suasion, and the implicit threat of non-nuclear military force. We must try to measure these more intangible forms of national power in order to see where the balance lies and which way it is shifting. The nuclear capability of last-resort use is a psychological factor of great effect in perceptions of strengths, but in most cases it is only one of the several elements of national power viewed as an instrument of policy, and then usually not the decisive factor.

Polarity, Geographic and Strategic

Much has been written in recent years about the passage of world affairs from an era of bipolarity (U.S.-Soviet conflict) to a condition of multipolarity. There is some truth in these assertions. Nations cluster together in groups such as those formed of the oil-rich, the industrially advanced, the economically disadvantaged, the strategically non-aligned. In many respects, however, the emphasis on multipolarity is dangerously wrong. The world is still, to a remarkable extent, divided between a sphere of influence dominated by the USSR and populated by states aligned politically and economically as well as militarily with the USSR, and a much less clearly delimited sphere of influence dominated—less firmly—by the United States and populated by states aligned with the United States economically or politically as well as in some cases through military pacts and guarantees.

There are many nations outside or not clearly associated with either of these spheres of influence, but the United States and the USSR—and particularly conflicts on varying levels of intensity between them—profoundly affect every other part of the globe. In this sense, despite the proliferation of smaller nations and the increase in strength of some of the secondary powers, the modern world is still fundamentally bipolar.

Perhaps a better way to put it is to say, in a strictly geographic sense, that the world is polar—because most of the continental land masses surround the North Pole. The great multicontinent Eurasia, containing 33 percent of the globe's land surface, lies totally within the northern hemisphere, and directly across the North Pole from it is the North American continent, comprising another 16 percent of the land surface of the earth.

The best way to examine the distribution of nations about the world is to look at a globe—not a flattened Mercator projection of it—and study it from a polar viewpoint, that is, literally by looking directly at the North Pole. The endpaper map conveyes the message. The United

9

States and the USSR confront each other across the north polar wastes, the two of them together comprising the largest agglomeration of choice temperate-zone territory and natural resources existing anywhere on earth.

Canada, in this strictly geographic sense, whether or not it likes the situation, becomes an important extension of the northern U.S. strategic border. Thus the geography of Canada impels its identification with North American security quite apart from the multiple economic and political ties between Canada and the United States, and indeed apart from the occasional frictions which arise between Washington and Ottawa. The Caribbean islands, Mexico, and Central America are strategically linked with the United States and with continental defense perimeters. This remains true even though these areas are also drawn culturally and politically toward South America and other regions (i.e., Britain, Spain, or France) and in some instances flaunt an anti-Yankee attitude on international issues.

Putting it crudely and literally, everything else in international affairs is peripheral; not unimportant but marginal to matters of primary strategic concern to the USSR and the United States. Other nations cluster in zones abutting on Soviet territory around the edges of the vast Eurasian continent; many nations are linked by sea-lanes to one another and to North America; some nations, of course, are pulled in both directions at once, and a few try to escape their natural geographic linkages by forming political bonds outside the broad zones in which they are situated. Thus we see Castro's Cuba anomalously linked to Moscow, and Albania similarly trying to reach out to Peking.

This basic polarity of North America and the Soviet heartland of Eurasia has long been apparent, but the nuclear missile age for the first time added enormous significance to the polar factor because it leaves the two continental superpowers locked in position just 30 minutes away from each other's military capability to destroy all the cities and most of the people in both countries. This power potential will probably never be used by either of the two deadly scorpions in the bottle, but all other international relationships are profoundly altered by it. The bipolar relationship between the United States and the USSR, both of which tend to dominate the regions of the earth in which they lie, is crucial to all international developments. The strength of these nations and the strengths of Zone I and Zone II are central to the world balance of power. The clustering of various nations, some voluntarily and some involuntarily, around the Soviet Union and the United States is the dominating feature of the international landscape of the second half of the twentieth century.

It is essential to remember that the strictly geographic substructure of international relationships is in many cases substantially modified by political and economic affinities or incompatibilities. Political traditions become cherished parts of national culture; among traditional cultures like calls to like and alien ideas are in general looked at askance. Trade ties that mutually benefit and enrich the lives of other people within bilateral or multilateral commercial systems are powerful forces pulling in the direction of cooperation. Conversely, competition for scarce raw materials or commodities or markets can breed bitter international enmities. Taking these complex economic and political factors together in a broad context, we find that there is another kind of polarity based on fundamental societal differences. Most modern nations can be classified somewhere along the spread of a novel but rather simple political spectrum reflecting major present-day tendencies, and when they are so arranged two clusters of associated nations appear at opposite sides of the horseshoe figure which best fits the facts.

Political and Economic Polarity

In laying out this spectrum, to avoid ethnocentrism or pejorative terms, I have deliberately avoided the conventional straight line classification based on left-right or conservative-liberal distinctions.

LEFT	CENTER	RIGHT
Revolutionary Radical	Liberal Conservative	Reactionary

These labels confuse, more often than clarify, today's political behavior groupings. A more useful way of describing modern political tendencies is to align societies along what I call the political horseshoe spectrum with the true opposites being pluralistic diversity and totalitarian conformity.

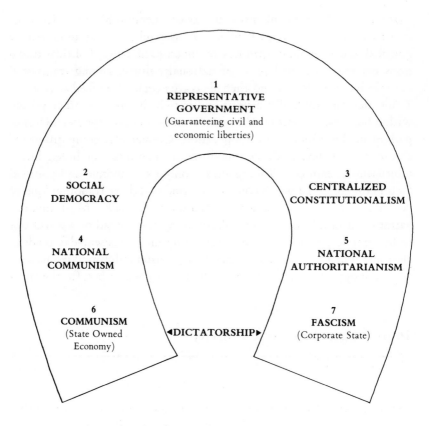

PLURALISM

1
REPRESENTATIVE
GOVERNMENT
(Guaranteeing civil and
economic liberties)

2
SOCIAL
DEMOCRACY

3
CENTRALIZED
CONSTITUTIONALISM

4
NATIONAL
COMMUNISM

5
NATIONAL
AUTHORITARIANISM

6
COMMUNISM
(State Owned
Economy)

◄**DICTATORSHIP**►

7
FASCISM
(Corporate State)

TOTALITARIANISM

1. The United States (presidential-congressional) and Great Britain (parliamentary) are archetypes of the two main varieties of representative government, both with constitutional guarantees of minority rights and electoral privileges.

2. West Germany is the best model of parliamentary social democracy in which a government assumes the obligation to manage the society to insure equal opportunity at minimum and some degree of egalitarianism at maximum.

3. France and Japan have highly centralized parliamentary regimes under rigid constitutional prescriptions and restraints.

4. Yugoslavia is the archetype of national Communism, struggling to be free from Soviet or Chinese domination; Vietnam emulates this model.

5. Many states of this kind exist, for example, Iran, and South Korea.

6. The Soviet Union and Mao Tse-tung's China are totalitarian Communist states.

7. Powerful fascist dictatorships of our era disappeared with Hitler and Mussolini, although there is no guarantee against their return. Some primitive dictatorships like Uganda under Idi Amin are almost as oppressive but lack the systematic use of state power to shape the economy and society positively as distinct from simply exercising arbitrary rule.

Looked at in this way on a broad political and economic spectrum, Central Eurasia and Communist Asia are the zones that contain states with one-party absolute dictatorships, closed societies, and autarkic command economies. These nations make up more than 25 percent of the world's land surface and contain about 35 percent of the world's population.

Despotism, tyranny, arbitrary rule without law—these forms of government have been all too common since men first began coming together in purposeful social groups. They are usually resorted to or tolerated out of despair of achieving any common social goals when individualism in constitutional or social democratic societies runs riot and borders on aimless anarchy.

In the twentieth century a new form of despotism has emerged, based on the superior technology of modern communications systems and police techniques. It calls for the total mobilization and control of people's actions and thoughts, thus moving a step beyond the passive obedience demanded by the great tyrannies of the past. There is no very good word to describe these new-style dictatorships, but totalitarian is most often used because it suggests the absolute, comprehensive character of the political control they seek. The models for such totalitarianism are Hitler's Germany, Stalin's Soviet Union, and Mao Tse-tung's China. They exhibit something new in their control techniques and something very old in their despotic forms of politics. Calling them dictatorships of the left or right is rather irrelevant. Their social control mechanisms and political theories are identical. In keeping with conventional left-right classifications they are separated by the open gap in the horseshoe figure, but in fact their political morals and methods are so similar that they can cooperate across the open end of the horseshoe when strategy demands it, as the Hitler-Stalin pact of 1939 demonstrated.

Along other parts of the spectrum near the closed end of the horseshoe are those societies which follow one of several middle courses steering between authority and liberty, between discipline and gratification of individual wishes, and, theoretically at least, between anarchy and effective government. At the center of this part of the spectrum is the group of societies that follow the pluralistic model of representative government, either parliamentary or presidential-congressional. The modern nation-states, in their five hundred years or so of evolution, have experimented with numerous political forms designed to give the benefits of social discipline without sacrificing the rights of individuals to pursue their happiness. The British evolved the system of resolving conflicts and sharing burdens and benefits through compromises arrived at in a representative parliament—by ballot rather than on the battlefield. The United States developed a variant with the separation of powers between executive and legislative authority. The emphasis in this kind of society is on toleration of diverse groups with different aims so long as they do not damage the common aims of the majority or plurality. The energy and initiatives originate among the citizens, with the government acting somewhat as umpire and sponsor of compromises likely to create a plurality in its support. It is the opposite of a totalitarian society, where the emphasis of government is on forcing goals and standards of behavior downwards on individuals and majority groups to conform with the decisions at the top. A final important distinction is that a pluralistic society includes among the rights of citizens the freedom to satisfy consumers' economic wants through private enterprise for private profit. This form of economic activity, with initiative coming from the bottom up, where it can be regulated if necessary, rather than from the top down, has always tended to lead to a private or corporate search for materials and markets outside national boundaries. Hence both the British and U.S. economies have stressed comparatively free international trade as well as protection of economic and political freedoms at home.

The United States and the major countries of West Europe, from which the largest part of the original U.S. population and cultural tradition stems, provide the most successful models for the kind of government that has clear limits on arbitrary rule, careful safeguards for election of representative leaders and legal protection for the right of minorities to exist safely together in the confines of a pluralistic state. Civil liberties, human rights, electoral privileges, representative government, and equality of economic opportunity are the hallmarks of these nations which, somewhat inexactly, label themselves democratic, whether social democracies, parliamentary systems, or presidential-congressional governments. The label "democratic" itself has become almost meaningless since it has been cynically appropriated and used by the Communist dictatorships; hence it is better to describe them as pluralistic, connoting tolerance of diverse population elements in the body politic in such nations, as well as the making of policy by shifting concentric pluralities which form a consensus for specific pragmatic purposes rather than by a fixed ideological goal.

Recent years have seen a shrinkage, rather than a growth, in the number of countries trying to follow the British-U.S. model of government. Classification of states along these lines is full of ambiguity, but it is probably valid as a broad generalization to say that only 20 percent of the four billion people in the world live in these kinds of relatively free, pluralistic national societies. This leaves about 45 percent of the world population in an in-between status, not free, not strictly totalitarian—ranging from non-Communist, often rather ineffective, authoritarian governments to nearly free but imperfect representative governments of various kinds, some of which are breaking down into near anarchy of the libertarian or egalitarian type usually called left and some of which avoid anarchy by turning to arbitrary authoritative rule.[4] Thus in political as well as geographic terms nations tend to cluster around two opposite poles, with a substantial group of relatively freer particles occupying a middle ground and being pulled in contrary directions. Polarity, both political and economic, is deeply imbedded in the politectonics of world power groupings.

It is frequently debated whether U.S. foreign policy should be based on considerations of international power or on political and moral precepts. Surely it should be based on both insofar as they are at all compatible. The decision-makers and the supporting public will be more united and more energetic if the moral concepts and political processes of the pluralistic society are reflected in policy decisions; prudence demands that power be taken into policy calculations at least sufficiently to guarantee the feasibility of the political course being taken. It is not really moral for a nation to pursue a principle that is impractical as a guide to coping with reality in the international arena. Total unrealism in world affairs, however high-minded, is not moral; it is a recipe for disaster. Consequently, in assessing alignments and frictions among nations it is necessary to examine the regional and structural distribution of nations, looking not only at the basic polarity just described but also at the idiosyncrasies and unusual characteristics of the nations which have escaped polarization.

Comparison by Politectonic Zones

The 158 nations of the world are scattered rather unevenly among the eleven politectonic zones identified in the following maps.

Zone I

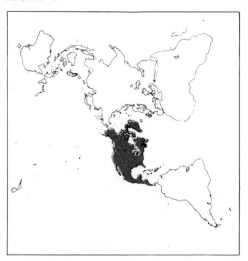

Bahamas
Barbados
Canada
Costa Rica
Dominican Republic
El Salvador
Grenada
Guatemala
Haiti
Honduras
Jamaica
Mexico
Nicaragua
Panama
Trinidad and Tobago
United States

Zone II

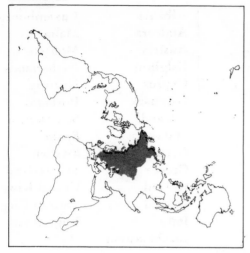

Bulgaria
Cuba
Czechoslovakia
Germany (GDR)
Hungary
Mongolia
Poland
Rumania
USSR

Zone III

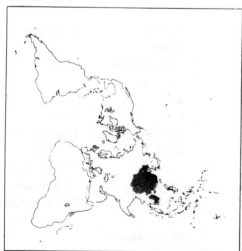

Cambodia
China (PRC)
North Korea
Laos
Vietnam

Zone IV

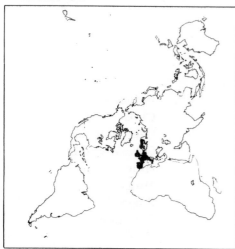

Albania	Luxembourg
Andorra	Malta
Austria	Monaco
Belgium	Netherlands
Cyprus	Norway
Denmark	Portugal
Finland	San Marino
France	Spain
Germany (FRG)	Sweden
Greece	Switzerland
Iceland	United Kingdom
Ireland	Vatican City
Italy	Yugoslavia
Liechtenstein	

Zone V

Algeria	Morocco
Bahrain	Oman
Cape Verde	Qatar
Egypt	Saudi Arabia
Iran	Sudan
Iraq	Syria
Israel	Tunisia
Jordan	Turkey
Kuwait	United Arab
Lebanon	Emirates
Libya	Yemen (Aden)
Mali	Yemen (Sana)
Mauritania	

Zone VI

Afghanistan
Bangladesh
Bhutan
India
Maldives
Nepal
Pakistan
Sri Lanka

Zone VII

Burma
Indonesia
Malaysia
Philippines
Singapore
Thailand

Zone VIII

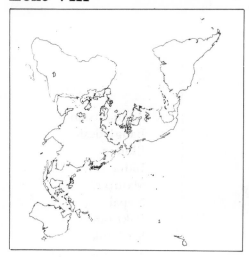

China/Taiwan
Japan
South Korea

Zone IX

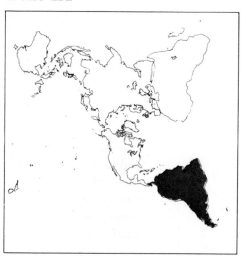

Argentina
Bolivia
Brazil
Chile
Colombia
Ecuador
Guyana
Paraguay
Peru
Surinam
Uruguay
Venezuela

Zone X

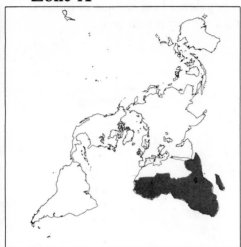

Angola
Benin
Botswana
Burundi
Cameroon
Central African
  Republic
Chad
Comoro Islands
Congo (Brazzaville)
Equatorial Guinea
Ethiopia
Gabon
Gambia
Ghana
Guinea
Guinea-Bissau
Ivory Coast
Kenya
Lesotho
Liberia
Madagascar

Malawi
Mauritius
Mozambique
Niger
Nigeria
Rhodesia
Rwanda
Sao Tome and
  Principe
Senegal
Seychelles
Sierra Leone
Somalia
South Africa
Swaziland
Tanzania
Togo
Uganda
Upper Volta
Zaire
Zambia

Zone XI

Australia
Fiji
Nauru
New Zealand
Papua New Guinea
Tonga
Western Samoa

Approximately four billion people are scattered around the roughly 52 million square miles of the earth's populated land surface as follows (omitting Antarctica's uninhabited six million square miles):

Zone	Population	Territory
	(millions rounded)	(millions of square miles, rounded)
I	333	9.3
II	375	9.6
III	1,025	4.0
IV	366	1.5
V	226	7.0
VI	824	2.0
VII	268	1.5
VIII	164	0.2
IX	216	6.8
X	304	6.6
XI	20	3.0

The North American Zone (I), which includes Central America and the Caribbean, except for Cuba, has a total land area of about 9.3 million square miles, which is 16 percent of the world total, and a population of about 333 million. It is a rich and productive region dominated by the United States because of that country's central location, its control of most of the temperate zone of the continent, and its large, productive population. Command of the Atlantic-Pacific sea passage via the Panama Canal adds an extra element of strategic importance to this zone.

Cuba is an anomaly, a fascinating example of a nation torn politically from its natural regional relationships and artificially aligned with the Soviet-dominated bloc of totalitarian states. In politectonic terms it is like an alien political volcano erupting in the Caribbean region of the North American Zone—pulled from its normal affinities into playing a military and economic role in conjunction with the Soviet Union. This pattern may become more common in the future if the USSR continues trying to reach out to establish influence over nations well outside the Eurasian heartland. Angola in Southern Africa comes to mind as an example where both Soviet and Cuban intervention have recently and radically altered strategic patterns in Southern Africa.

Zone II is a little over 9.6 million square miles in area, of which the greatest part (8.6 million) lies within the USSR. Mongolia accounts for most of the remainder, while the six East European Communist states plus Cuba add up to less than one-half million square miles. The total population of these Zone II states, including Cuba, is about 375 million. It is rich and productive, especially in the temperate zone of the Soviet Union and in the Central European heartland. Strategically the central land mass, which touches on much of the peninsular and insular part of Eurasia, is in a dominant position, its greatest weakness being geographic and climatic limitations on access to the oceans. Because of the size of the USSR and its method of government, the 130 million or so Great Russians in the USSR exercise greater influence over the peoples and resources of this whole zone (II) than the 215 million people in the United States exercise in Zone I. In fact the USSR is the only truly imperial power in the world today, since the Great Russians totally dominate the other Slavs, the numerous non-Slav peoples of the trans-Caucasus and Inner Asia, and the East Europeans.

The Asian Communist Zone (III) is still another continent-sized region dominated strategically by a single country, the People's Republic of China. North Korea and North Vietnam maintain some independence of action by keeping their political lines to Moscow open, but the cultural backgrounds of their populations and their geographical proximity draw this entire region toward the PRC. Vietnam, while apprehensive about being pulled into a Peking-dominated hegemony, has its hands full organizing the recently conquered territory of South Vietnam politically and economically. The reunified Vietnam governed from Hanoi is now dominant in Laos, Cambodia having fallen more directly into the Chinese orbit. Vietnam will be obliged to cooperate with China for some time to come, but is leaning more strongly toward Moscow to counterbalance its obligations to Peking. The whole zone (III) bulks very large in East Asia. It covers about four million square miles of territory and sustains a population of over one billion people, most of them in China, constituting one-fourth of the world's total population.

The friction at the edges of politectonic zones is nowhere better illustrated than in the case of Communist Asia. The dispute between China (PRC) and the USSR over the 4,500-mile border between the two countries and over Mongolia, now thoroughly incorporated in the Soviet political and economic system, is a perennial source of conflict, and actual fighting breaks out periodically along the Amur River and in Sinkiang.

Furthermore, both China and Vietnam are supporting revolutionary movements and guerrilla forces in the bordering Southeast Asian states: Burma, Thailand, and Malaysia. Where Peking-controlled Tibet meets India's client states across the Himalayas, border disputes and bitter political conflict have been going on for 15 or 20 years. The initial cordiality between Indian Prime Minister Nehru and PRC Prime Minister Chou En-lai broke down abruptly when the Chinese attacked Indian armies on the frontier in 1962 and administered a quick, thorough defeat to Indian defense forces. Hostility has been constant since that time. Politectonic drift and peripheral clashes appear inevitable when adjoining zones are dominated by powers with different cultures, different social and political systems, and markedly different world views. The tension and instability on the entire periphery of Eurasia demonstrate this strategic fact of life.

Proceeding counterclockwise around Eurasia, the first peninsular region is West Europe. At times high hopes have been held for a political evolution that would unite many of these nations into a single community organized for security, economic interchange, and political legislation. Today this concept is still far from becoming a reality, and the states of West Europe take on a common identity mainly by their common economic system (EEC) and by their sheltering within the North Atlantic Pact defense system. Zone IV, then, is made up of those states not incorporated in the autocratic Soviet system that embraces East Germany and East Europe. It is a small region, but its population is substantial and has produced technology and living standards as high as, or higher than, any in the world today.

In this region, as defined here, 27 states are included, ranging from the Vatican City (population 1,000 on one and one-half square miles), Andorra, Liechtenstein, and Malta, on the smaller side, to France, Germany, the United Kingdom, Italy, and Spain, on the larger. Zone IV has a total area of about one and one-half million square miles with a population of a little over 366 million. Because of common ethnic backgrounds and cultural affinities, West Europe lines up with North America without drastic friction in most matters, thus constituting the bizonal association usually called the Atlantic community. The political symbolism of this concept and the practical defense arrangements of the North Atlantic Treaty are primary features in present-day international affairs.

On the other hand, West Europe borders on Zone II along an entirely artificial line through Central Europe where Soviet armies and Soviet policy stopped at the end of the 1940s—Churchill's "Iron Curtain." This has been a conflict-prone border ever since, with a focal point of tension in West Berlin and periodic trouble in a divided Germany. The people of both Czechoslovakia and Hungary have had to be suppressed by Soviet armies to prevent those countries from deviating from the Soviet political model or from being drawn into the West European cluster of states, with which East Europe has many ties.

On the western side of the "Iron Curtain" the appeal of Eurocommunism to substantial elements of the population in Italy, France, and Portugal has caused political turbulence that is unsettling to parliamentary regimes in those states, although the Eurocommunists act more independently of the USSR than Moscow likes. The politectonic rift line where Zone II and Zone IV meet is inherently unstable. There are two states along this Central European border which have doggedly resisted inclusion in the Soviet sphere of influence, while remaining under domestic Communist Party dictatorships and holding aloof from West Europe. They are Yugoslavia, which escaped Soviet controls in the Stalin era to become subsequently steadfastly "neutral," and Albania, which leans on Peking to preserve its independence from the West, from Yugoslavia, and from the Soviet Union. For purely geographic reasons, and because of their determination to stay out of Soviet clutches, these states are included as marginally part of West Europe. In terms of political structure and behavior, Yugoslavia is more akin to Zone II and Albania is more akin to its Chinese ally in Zone III.

The North African states and those of the Mideast constitute a politectonic zone (V) separated by the Mediterranean and Black Seas, on one side, and the Sahara Desert, on the other, from bordering regions. Its diversity is greater than its unity, but religion (Islam) and a sense of Pan-Arabism tie various parts of it together. One of the larger states, Iran, is in fact not Arab at all; instead it inherits and emulates the cultural tradition and pride of ancient Persia. The state which creates

most of the tension in the area by its very existence is Israel. It is small but dynamic and its Hebraic heritage sets its inhabitants off sharply from the other Semitic peoples of the area.

The tribalism and complex history of Zone V are reflected in the number of separate states which comprise it, many of them very small. This zone lies at the crossroads of Asia, Europe, and Africa, and contains the strategic Suez link between the Mediterranean and the Indian Ocean. It has probably been the most fought-over region of the world since the days of ancient Egypt and the Roman Empire. Now, of course, its enormous oil reserves inevitably make the Mideast a ripe plum for contesting influences from powerful industrial states in neighboring politectonic zones.

The African area between the Sahara and the Mediterranean, basically Arab in background, contains nine states with a population of about 100 million and territory, not very hospitable or productive for the most part, amounting to about four million square miles. In the Arabian Peninsula itself there are 12 states (counting the United Arab Emirates as one), with a population of about 40 million and territory amounting to a little less than two million square miles, one-third of which belongs to the six million people of Saudi Arabia. This region contains by far the greatest petroleum deposits available anywhere in the world.

Turkey, Israel, and Iran are each culturally distinct although geographically situated in the Mideast. Their populations of 40.9 million, 3.5 million, and 34 million, respectively, live within territorial boundaries comprising about 300 thousand square miles, 8 thousand square miles, and 636 thousand square miles. In total, Zone V supports a population of about 226 million on a little less than 7 million square miles of land, much of it desert.

The subcontinent of South Asia with the adjacent ocean area is a politectonic zone (VI) in the most literal sense. Geologically it drifted from a more southerly location millions of years ago and collided with Asia, uplifting the Himalayas which still separate it from Central Asia. It comprises only eight states, including a mini-state, the Maldives. The Zone VI population reaches the staggering total of about 824 million, the majority of which is situated in India, on a total territory of about 2 million square miles. Friction along the northern and eastern politectonic borders is endemic.

What is left of Southeast Asia, Zone VII, once Indochina has been separated in accord with its political coloration and treated as part of Communist Asia, is largely an island territory of nearly one and one-half million square miles supporting a population of about 268 million. Indonesia has approximately one-half of the people and land in the six countries in Zone VII.

Here the fault line separating the mainland states of Zone VII from Zone III to the north is unstable, and this has been the most turbulent zone of recent years because of the conflict which ended only in 1975 with the severing of South Vietnam, Cambodia, and Laos from this grouping of states and the effective establishment of North Vietnamese or Chinese hegemony over these 30-odd millions of people and 225 thousand square miles of fertile subtropical territory. The borders of these Indochina states with their Zone VII neighbors are rather permeable and unsettled in view of clashing interests and ideologies. The control of the narrow passages between the Pacific and Indian Oceans by Indonesia and Singapore give these nations and this politectonic zone special strategic significance.

The remaining peripheral region of Eurasia, Zone VIII, is a small but politically and geographically disparate cluster of three states: Japan, South Korea, and China/Taiwan. Its total population is about 164 million and its territory only about 195 thousand square miles. It constitutes a pivotal strategic triangle, each point of which interlocks with the others, and the whole sits in the center of a larger triangle where mainland Chinese, Soviet Far Eastern, and U.S. Pacific interests meet. It is stable in the special sense of being under such great tension from all sides, like the capstone in a vaulted arch, that a major change of structural strategic position in any part of Northeast Asia would undermine the security of the area and tend to destabilize the relationship of the larger powers, none of which at present appears anxious for this to happen.

An unanticipated or unavoidable political or strategic change in any of the three countries in Zone VIII could cause the region to disintegrate. The danger of such destabilization is high throughout the zone. China/Taiwan is a politically cohesive nation of nearly 16 million people, but its territory is claimed by the Communist regime in Peking which ousted the government of the Republic of China (China/Taiwan) in 1949. While Peking probably does not want to incur the risks and costs of trying to take the island now, it has made "liberate Taiwan" one of its most constantly reiterated slogans. The Chinese people living in Taiwan have a standard of economic well-being over three times as high as that on the mainland and a considerably less autocratic form of government. They have no intention of succumbing to Communist rule if they can help it. Both Taipei and Peking believe there is only one China, which each feels it should rightly, *de jure,* govern; in reality, *de facto,* they are two independent states of a divided nation and are likely to remain so for some time.

South Korea is also part of a divided country, in this case a more equitably divided one. North Korea, with Soviet and Chinese Communist support, tried to unify the peninsula by military force in 1950 and still threatens to do so. South Korea is strong enough and politically coherent enough to fight against any attack from the North, so long as it can count on military assistance from the United States. Since the Korean peninsula as a whole has long been perceived as a dagger pointing at the heart of Japan, the Japanese have every interest in maintaining the present status quo.

Japan, also, appears to be able to sustain the enormous pressures on this region so long as it remains part of the U.S.-Pacific security system. It has little military strength, but its level of economic development carries great influence throughout East Asia, and the great size of its population makes it the northern equivalent of Indonesia in the long chain of islands that flank the continent along an arc nearly 3,000 miles in length. The whole sweep of West Pacific insular nations constitutes a great strategic barrier, dividing the largely ocean-oriented Pacific basin from the continental nations. Because this barrier arc is a key element in the security of Pacific-Indian Ocean sea-lanes, it constitutes a strategic prize of great value to the major powers.

Most of these first eight politectonic zones are in the northern hemisphere. In the water-filled southern hemisphere, on the outer crescent of the globe as viewed on the polar map, are three politectonic zones whose strategic fate is ultimately tied up with the evolution of power in the Eurasian and North American zones. At this point in history they are beginning to exert considerable leverage in the international arena although the power position of even the leading nations in these outer zones is as yet relatively limited. Their potential importance is enormous, and the way they evolve in this decade will unquestionably foreshadow the ultimate role they play in strategic global conflicts.

These three zones are designated, rather arbitrarily, as Latin America south of Panama, Central and Southern Africa below the Sahara, and the South Pacific island region of Australia and New Zealand, which includes Fiji, Nauru, Papua New Guinea, Tonga, and Western Samoa. The significance of geography, political coherence, and economic development is nowhere so dramatically illustrated as in the comparatively restricted role played in world affairs by Zones IX, X, and XI, which collectively include nations with about 500 million people in them and a total land area of over 16 million square miles. Because they are in comparatively remote locations from one another and from the northern hemisphere countries, and because until recently they have had only limited economic and political leverage, these outer crescent nations enter into global strategic considerations mainly when they ally themselves or become embroiled in disputes with the larger powers of the northern hemisphere. As sources of many valuable raw materials essential to the industrial nations of the world, however, these zones are becoming more and more important.

A Politectonic Strategy for Americans—1977

This book views the complex international scene just described in politectonic terms from the viewpoint of Washington, where the security and the political goals of the U.S. body politic are primary objectives in national policymaking. International behavior patterns and trends are kaleidoscopic, baffling. It is essential to focus on fundamentals if we are to formulate sound national strategy and pursue a sensible policy in dealing with other states. In a study of foreign policy written during World War II, Walter Lippmann laid down as a "fundamental principle" the need of "bringing into balance, with a comfortable surplus of power in reserve, the nation's commitments and the nation's power." He went on to say that "the true statesman" must be sure that commitments concerning "ideals, interests, and ambitions which are to be asserted abroad" are covered or balanced by adequate support at home "combined with the support he can find abroad among other nations which have similar ideals, interests, and ambitions."[5] In other words, if the United States is to balance its foreign policy commitments with its national power, alliances with overseas nations are crucial. Key nations in the global politectonic structure must be preserved lest the crumbling of some destroy the foundations on which others rest.

Every citizen is entitled to have his own prescription for a redefined U.S. strategy that would win national support and permit the United States to conduct a foreign policy in pursuit of a favorable balance in its international relations. From my viewpoint, reflecting the analysis developed in this study of world power, the most promising strategic blueprint for the 1970s and 1980s would be a select system of trans-oceanic alliances formed or reconfirmed on a voluntary basis by strong nations strategically located and linked by common political, economic, and security interests with the United States. The model ought to be the Athenian League of the fifth century B.C. which defeated the onslaught of the armies sent by Persia's tyrants to conquer Greece. The Athenian League's use of seapower and the voluntary fiscal contributions, as well as the ships and fighting men, of allied Greek city-states permitted the mobilization of military forces which were more dynamic and better led than the pirates they swept from the seas as well as superior to the armies of the much more powerful absolute monarchy the Greeks were fighting in that time.

For many years the Athenian League experienced remarkable success in keeping peace and protecting commerce in the whole Eastern Mediterranean. The wellsprings of much of what we consider civilization arise from this era. Only later did the states of the League fall to bickering among themselves over burden-sharing, and Athens attempted to use naked force against her own allies to hold them together rather than work out clear common policy purposes that would guarantee voluntary cooperation. In these circumstances the alliance fell into disrepair and its ill-conceived and badly managed military ventures eventually destroyed it, along with the fortunes of all its member states.

What is needed now in the aftermath of the American Age of the 1950s and 1960s is to reconstitute a pattern of key alliances—a kind of latter-day Athenian League—on the basis of informed common understanding of the problems ahead. Such a group must be strong enough to counter hostile moves by potential adversaries, particularly the totalitarian states which are hostile to U.S. society as a matter of principle. The aim of the United States should be to select and work closely with the main allies with whom we share a number of interests and strategic aims. The ultimate goal is not imperial hegemony but a common dedication to insuring the safety and desired way of political and social life of these nations' respective citizens. To evoke the best and most realistic aspirations of the people in each society is the real role of national strategy.

Today what the United States needs is a consensus in support of a non-totalitarian alliance capable of maintaining an approximation of the present balance of world power. The right alliance at this time can stop unfavorable trends. It can only be a strictly voluntary association of a core group of friendly states, committed to a mutually beneficial cooperation with each other in economic relations, in military burden-sharing, and in political planning. Its goals would embrace the essential purposes of the North Atlantic community, but its scope would be broader geographically and its functions would extend beyond military planning to political and economic cooperation. The alliance would prove itself by equitably sharing out the benefits of comparatively free trade among the interdependent industrial nations and other states whose raw material resources are essential to a decent standard of living for all.

Other states should be viewed as potential associates of individual members of such a core group, and not as adversaries, unless they choose to be. The pluralistic tradition that allows minority rights within nations ought to make possible the toleration of considerable political and cultural diversity among nations linked together for common security and economic cooperation. The numerous nations of the so-called Third World may join such an alliance if they accept the common strategy or live in harmony with it. A reasonable amount of economic aid to all needy nations on the basis of a common humanity ought to be one of the stabilizing policies of the alliance. It is unrealistic, however, to expect the poorer and less powerful nations to carry the burdens or take the risks of major allies. Many political and social changes will from time to time disrupt the power potential of the hundred-odd weaker states. Not all of today's nations will survive, since local and tribal loyalties are strong and divisive in many regions, and ancient enmities survive in countless forms. The leading nations, however, comprising the core group of the stronger pluralist societies, must stick together firmly in maintaining something close to the balance of power of the mid-1970s, or better. Otherwise all of them will suffer individual losses of security and influence adding up to an irreparable shift toward totalitarian domination and away from a world free for diversity.

The best name I can think of for such an association of independent nations is "Oceans Alliance," in reference to the Atlantic, Pacific, and Indian seaways which link these states. In a global sense there is only one world ocean, surrounding Eurasia and connecting the peripheral nations of the Eurasian rimland with the Americas. The many other international associations in which the United States participates could continue as at present, but the predominant strategic aim of the cluster of states forming an Oceans Alliance structure would simply be to bind themselves to cultivate transoceanic economic interdependence and transoceanic cooperation in support of the common security of these pluralist societies.

Such a strategy for the United States is implicit in the whole situation described in the pages of this book. It is closely related to the old U.S. national strategy of the 1950s and 1960s. The new strategy might be formulated along these lines:

The United States should protect the security of its people and society by maintaining an alliance system of nations with non-totalitarian societies which will prevent a totalitarian nation or combination of such nations from establishing political or military control over all of central Eurasia (the region now controlled by the USSR) *plus* any substantial parts of the Eurasian peripheral rimlands.

To translate this strategy into the politectonic terminology employed in this book, this strategy would mean: the USSR and China can expect peaceful relations with the United States provided they do not try to dominate from their central (heartland) position in Eurasia any of the major countries in the peripheral Zones IV through VIII, that is, in West Europe, North Africa and the Mideast, South Asia, Southeast Asia, and Northeast Asia. In the case of direct or indirect aggression by either the USSR or the PRC or both against any of the major nations which voluntarily join an Oceans Alliance, the United States would render political, economic, logistic, and, if necessary, military assistance to the extent that circumstances required. Such commitments would have to be guaranteed by agreements or treaties approved by the U.S. Senate. They would have to be understood by the citizens of the United States as basic to their own security and prosperity.

Existing U.S. alliance commitments would not necessarily be dropped if the President and the Congress could agree on a new affirmation of strategic purpose along these lines and invite the major nations to shoulder special responsibility in pursuit of this strategy. The NATO alliance could continue as an overlapping security system. Smaller members of NATO such as Portugal, Greece, the participating Scandinavian countries, and Iceland, regardless of size and power, would be eligible to join the Oceans Alliance if they chose to adopt its purposes.

In any case, decisive leadership in the United States in pursuit of a clearly articulated strategic goal of this kind could bring together an association of nations worthy of the description of a new Athenian League and capable of preventing the spread of Soviet or Chinese—and certainly Vietnamese or North Korean—forms of totalitarianism. It is clear that at this stage of the historical evolution of international politics it is not possible to "leave it to the UN" or to other existing organizations to preserve a stable world order.[6] The United States must instead implement the purposes of the UN Charter—which are excellent as abstract goals—with the moral force, political purpose, and military power necessary to protect the way of life of the pluralist nations of the world. The nature of this undertaking and the specifics of nations and national power involved comprise the subject matter of the remainder of this book.

Measuring the Power of Nations

Obviously a sound U.S. strategy requires an objective calculus of national power and clusters of power in the international arena. This calculus must include an analysis of nuclear weaponry and its potential for the deterrence of war, but other elements of strength constitute crucial factors. Non-nuclear arms and forces, economic capacity, and economic resources materially affect the way national power is perceived and hence its effect. Coherence in formulating concepts of national purpose and the degree of consensus expressed as political will substantially alter the way military and economic power can be used.

National power, realistically described, is a mix of strategic, military, economic, and political strengths and weaknesses. It is determined in part by the military forces and the military establishment of a country but even more by the size and location of territory, the nature of frontiers, the populations, the raw-material resources, the economic structure, the technological development, the financial strength, the ethnic mix, the social cohesiveness, the stability of political processes and decision-making, and, finally, the intangible quantity usually described as national spirit.

To ease the task of describing elements of international power in their various combinations, I have evolved a formula relating these factors. It is not a magic measuring rod, for many of the variables are not truly quantifiable. It simply provides a shorthand notation or index system to replace words and judgments once these have been defined.

The formula is as follows:

$$P_p = (C + E + M) \times (S + W)$$

Its terms are defined thus:

P_p = **Perceived Power**
C = **Critical Mass = Population + Territory**
E = **Economic Capability**
M = **Military Capability**
S = **Strategic Purpose**
W = **Will to Pursue National Strategy**

All of these terms will become clearer as we manipulate our observations within this conceptual framework for measuring real power in the international arena.

It only takes a careful look at the size and state of the economic development of the nations of the world to realize that the majority of them have relatively little impact on international affairs or even on important developments in their own regions. In a serious strategic assessment, only about 40 to 50 nations determine the pattern of the world balance of power at any one time. The rest either weigh so little in realistic power terms that they can disregarded, or perhaps viewed as the political equivalent of iron filings, automatically arranging them-selves around magnetic fields of force in the geographic zones or alliance systems to which they belong.

This is not to say the people of the less powerful countries are unimportant or that long-range strategic and humanitarian concerns can be ignored, especially since these also motivate citizens and governments. Yet, by any consistent standards of gross measurement, the preponderance of power appears to be in the hands of a relatively few nations.

Actually some very simple quantifications appear to be adequate for the rough approximations of strength in world affairs on which most broad generalizations about the balance of power rest. We are dealing here in macrometrics, the technique of measuring in a broad context where precise detail is not very significant. The patterns and trends in international relationships are what we want to see, not the details; the forest, not the trees.

In the same vein, index numbers are used to weight values and quantify strengths in this book. They reflect subjective and, in a sense, arbitrary judgments based on broad perceptions. They are used to convey easily and manipulate arithmetically estimates of comparative strengths and weaknesses among nations and groups of nations. It is crucial in using this calculus to understand that we are talking about perceptions of power by governments, which are often influenced by popular perceptions, and not necessarily about concrete elements of usable power. Power capable of being used seldom changes rapidly, but perceptions of it are volatile, particularly in societies where public opinion is important and ideas circulate freely. Many of the judgments in this book may need to be changed substantially as situations change, and particularly if the perceptions of these situations change. The macrometric values assigned in the following pages generally fit and also reflect the conventional perceptions of world power as it is viewed in 1977.

CHAPTER TWO

Critical Mass:
Population and Territory
$P_p = (C + E + M) \times (S + W)$

T he first factor in the formula for measuring perceived power in international affairs is what I have called critical mass (C), a judgment on the size or mass of a nation. This perception is often blurred or diffuse, but it is fundamentally based on the amount of territory under a state's control and the number of people supported economically by that territory. While it is hard to quantify, there does seem to be a kind of critical mass—a reflection of population and area—that a nation must ordinarily possess to make itself felt in world affairs.

In view of these age-old facts, we begin our measurement effort with this crude oversimplification: $P_p = C$. Obviously additional factors and coefficients are needed to make a more accurate formula for perceived power. It is revealing, nevertheless, to make a first approximation of the strength of nations in the international balance in this traditional way.

Population[1]

The first factor to look at in considering the importance of states is people. It is the sense of community among human beings that identifies the nation-state and infuses it with life. People exploit the raw economic resources of the territory they live in and develop the political and social traditions that shape national cultures. The spirit and competence of the individual human beings in a society, in the long run, may count as much as or more than the concrete and material resources a nation possesses.

The Table of Countries below, arranged in order of their population size, shows that 90 percent of the roughly 4 billion people in the world live in countries which have a population of 15 million or more. There are just 42 countries of this size. In fact, approximately one-half of the population of the world resides in the four largest countries, China, India, the USSR, and the United States. Population size is clearly a major element in international perceptions of whether or not a country constitutes a critical mass in terms of national power.

It is true that a few countries with small populations—Israel, Saudi Arabia, Singapore, and New Zealand, for example—have a dispro-portionate influence in international affairs because of some special circumstance, such as strategic location or some other factor, that can be identified under another term in our equation. But it is hard to think of most of the nations with a population of less than 15 million as having truly great power in their own right, independent of the interests or actions of other larger nations. In some cases, especially China, India, and, above all, Bangladesh, a large population may be a mixed blessing; it is nonetheless true that the sheer mass of 15 million people or more constitutes a force to be reckoned with, and the 15 nations with populations over 50 million include most of the countries commonly perceived as world powers. The People's Republic of China, India, the Soviet Union, the United Kingdom, Italy, and France—these are the countries to whose policies and fortunes the international community always pays heed. Altogether the 42 most heavily populated states have within their borders more than three and one-half billion, or nine-tenths, of the world's inhabitants. These 42 nations, each with more than 15 million people within its borders, are certainly "more equal" than all the rest.

From the viewpoint of assessing what I have called the critical mass of countries, it is useful to arrange them into ranklists weighted according to both population and area. For this purpose an arbitrary scale of 100 permits the nations to be rated in comparable size groupings, with equal importance (maximum of 50 points) being attached to predominance in numbers of people or in extent of territory.[2]

The first step then is to make a list including the most populous nations in order of descending size, with weights attached from 50 down to 10 according to groups with arbitrary breakpoints in size of population selected purely for convenience. Nations with populations under 15 million are awarded no weight in this ranklist system.

Population: 42 Largest Countries

Countries	Population (millions)	Perceived Power Weight
1. China (PRC)*	951	
2. India*	628	50
3. USSR	257	
4. United States	215	
5. Indonesia*	134	
6. Japan	113	45
7. Brazil	110	
8. Bangladesh*	76	
9. Pakistan*	73	
10. Nigeria	65	
11. West Germany (FRG)	62	40
12. Mexico	62	
13. United Kingdom	56	
14. Italy	56	
15. France	53	
16. Vietnam	46	
17. Philippines	44	
18. Thailand	44	
19. Turkey	41	30
20. Egypt	38	
21. Spain	36	
22. South Korea	35	
23. Poland	34	
24. Iran	34	

*These nations with very high populations and very low per capita GNP (over 50 million and under $300) at present suffer from the economic burden of large impoverished populations more than they benefit from the manpower. Nevertheless, in common perceptions very large populations cause countries to be taken seriously by other nations. For example, the People's Republic of China, weak in most regards other than population, is treated as a great power almost universally.

Countries	Population (millions)	Perceived Power Weight
25. Burma	31	
26. Ethiopia	28.6	25
27. South Africa	26.2	
28. Argentina	25.7	
29. Zaire	25.5	
30. Canada	23.1	
31. Colombia	22.9	20
32. Yugoslavia	21.5	
33. Rumania	21.4	
34. Afghanistan	19.5	
35. Sudan	18.2	
36. Morocco	17.9	
37. Algeria	17.3	
38. North Korea	17.0	10
39. East Germany (GDR)	16.8	
40. China/Taiwan	16.2	
41. Peru	15.8	
42. Tanzania	15.5	

Population: Remaining Countries

Country	Population
Under 15 Million	
Czechoslovakia	14.9
Sri Lanka	14.0
Kenya	13.8
Netherlands	13.7
Australia	13.6
Under 13 Million	
Nepal	12.8
Venezuela	12.3
Malaysia	12.3
Under 12 Million	
Uganda	11.9
Iraq	11.3
Hungary	10.6
Chile	10.4
Ghana	10.1

Country	Population
Under 10 Million	
Belgium	9.8
Cuba	9.4
Mozambique	9.2
Greece	9.0
Under 9 Million	
Bulgaria	8.8
Portugal	8.7
Sweden	8.2
Under 8 Million	
Cambodia	7.8
Malagasy Republic	7.7
Austria	7.5
Syria	7.5
Ecuador	7.0
Under 7 Million	
Ivory Coast	6.9
Yemen (Sana)	6.7
Cameroon	6.5
Rhodesia	6.5
Switzerland	6.4
Angola	6.2
Saudi Arabia	6.2
Upper Volta	6.1
Guatemala	6.0
Under 6 Million	
Tunisia	5.9
Mali	5.7
Bolivia	5.5
Malawi	5.1
Denmark	5.0
Under 5 Million	
Zambia	4.9
Dominican Republic	4.8
Finland	4.7
Niger	4.7
Haiti	4.6
Guinea	4.5
Senegal	4.3

Country	Population
Rwanda	4.3
El Salvador	4.1
Chad	4.1
Norway	4.0

Under 4 Million

Burundi	3.8
Israel	3.5
Laos	3.4
Somalia	3.2
New Zealand	3.1
Benin (formerly Dahomey)	3.1
Ireland	3.1

Under 3 Million

Honduras	2.8
Papua New Guinea	2.7
Sierra Leone	2.7
Jordan	2.7
Uruguay	2.7
Paraguay	2.6
Lebanon	2.5
Libya	2.5
Albania	2.4
Singapore	2.2
Togo	2.2
Nicaragua	2.2
Jamaica	2.0
Costa Rica	2.0

Under 2 Million

Central African Republic	1.8
Panama	1.7
Liberia	1.5
Mongolia	1.4
Congo (Brazzaville)	1.3
Mauritania	1.3
Bhutan	1.2
Lesotho	1.0
Trinidad and Tobago	1.0
Kuwait	1.0

Country

Under 1 Million
Mauritius
Guyana
Cyprus
Botswana
Fiji
Gabon
Gambia
Guinea-Bissau
Oman
Swaziland
Yemen (Aden)

Under 500 Thousand
Comoro Islands
Luxembourg
Malta
Equatorial Guinea
Cape Verde Islands
Barbados
Bahrain
Iceland
Bahamas
United Arab Emirates
Qatar
Western Samoa
Maldives
Tonga
Surinam

Under 100 Thousand
Liechtenstein
Monaco
Andorra
San Marino
Nauru
Sao Tome and Principe
Sechelles
Grenada

Under 1 Thousand
Vatican City

Territory

Land area is also basic to our weighting system of critical mass. The distribution of territory among nations is as inequitable as the distribution of population. In general, although not in every case, large territory means ample raw material resources for a people to exploit economically.[3] There are approximately 58 million square miles of land surface in the world (versus about 140 million square miles of ocean surface). If the "big boys" with one-half million square miles or more of territory each are selected out, they have nearly two-thirds of the total land mass of the globe.

The "big boys" in this sense number just 17 nations:

Country	Thousands of Square Miles
1. USSR	8,600
2. Canada	3,850
3. China (PRC)	3,700
4. United States	3,620
5. Brazil	3,290
6. Australia	2,970
7. India	1,210
8. Argentina	1,070
9. Sudan	970
10. Algeria	950
11. Zaire	900
12. Saudi Arabia	900
13. Mexico	760
14. Indonesia	740
15. Libya	680
16. Iran	640
17. Mongolia	600

It is true that the three biggest countries have enormous areas that are waste, desert, or are otherwise ill-suited for any kind of cultivation. Only about 26 percent of the Soviet Union's territory is arable, cultivated, or natural pastureland, while much of the rest is permafrost. Canada has even less arable or cultivated land (6 percent) and China little more (11 percent). This factor scales these giants down in size considerably so that they roughly match the United States, which has nearly half (46 percent) of its territory in arable land or cultivated pasture. Thus the big four are on a level by themselves. Not far behind, on another level of size, Australia, India, and Argentina have almost half or more of their land cultivated or arable; Brazil has the smallest amount in this group at 17 percent.

A number of these very large countries occupying more than one-half million square miles of territory happen to have enormous desert areas within their boundaries; all of them except Australia, Saudi Arabia, Libya, and Mongolia are on the list of the 42 most populous nations, reaching critical mass in the eyes of the world for this reason as well as territorial size. If our territorial ranklist is extended further down to include the United Kingdom, which is surely perceived by nearly everyone as a nation of consequence, territorially as well as in population, the cutoff point would then be fixed to include 71 nations, each controlling territory of 94 thousand square miles or more. These 71 nations occupy nearly 80 percent of the land surface of the globe.

Of these 71, many (35) have a population of less than 15 million, and some of them much less. Since quite a few of the larger territories are desert or waste, a small population may mean the country cannot be developed into a modern, powerful nation, or that the prospect is still a long way off. In the special case of Saudi Arabia the strategic and economic value of its petroleum resources insures international power in keeping with its territorial size despite the desert character of most of its land and the small size of its population. Each nation is a separate case, but perceptions reflect the crude facts of territorial extent as one determining factor in establishing the critical mass of a country.

Some other nations, not so large, control particularly important land or sea corridors, such as the Suez Canal, the Bosporus and the Strait of Malacca. Still others have achieved considerable impact because of control of valuable natural resources or by developing special economic skills or commodities which are in demand in international trade. In the following chart a bonus value is added for occupation of crucial strategic locations; economic bonus values are reserved for special weighting in the calculus of economic capabilities in the next chapter. Nevertheless, leaving these special cases aside, large area, if accompanied by a large population, almost automatically confers the status of power and will be so interpreted by strategists both at home and abroad. This image of status or power is what I call critical mass. The eight largest nations geographically have populations of over 15 million except for Australia; with only 13 1/2 million people, Australia is a marginal member of this top group, sustained in it by the impression of having vast natural resources to exploit as the population grows. These eight are perceived by all as consequential nations.

Territory: 71 Major Countries

	Country	Square Miles		Perceived Power Weight
1.	USSR	8.6 m.		
2.	Canada	3.9 m.		50
3.	China (PRC)	3.7 m.		
4.	United States	3.6 m.		
5.	Brazil	3.3 m.		
6.	Australia	3.0 m.		40
7.	India	1.2 m.		
8.	Argentina	1.1 m.		
9.	Sudan	970 th.		
10.	Algeria	950 th.		
11.	Zaire	900 th.		
12.	Saudi Arabia	900 th.		
13.	Mexico	760 th.		30
14.	Indonesia*	740 th.	(35)	
15.	Libya	680 th.		
16.	Iran*	640 th.	(35)	
17.	Mongolia	600 th.		
18.	Chad	496 th.		
19.	Peru	496 th.		
20.	Niger	490 th.		
21.	Angola	481 th.		
22.	South Africa*	470 th.	(25)	
23.	Mali	470 th.		20
24.	Ethiopia	460 th.		
25.	Colombia	440 th.		
26.	Bolivia	420 th.		
27.	Mauritania	420 th.		

*A bonus weight value of 5 points is added for nations occupying crucial strategic locations on sea lanes.

	Country	Square Miles		Perceived Power Weight
28.	Egypt*	390 th.	(25)	
29.	Tanzania	360 th.		
30.	Nigeria	360 th.		
31.	Venezuela	350 th.		
32.	Pakistan	310 th.		
33.	Mozambique	300 th.		20
34.	Turkey*	300 th.	(25)	
35.	Chile	290 th.		
36.	Zambia	290 th.		
37.	Burma	260 th.		
38.	Afghanistan	250 th.		
39.	Somalia*	240 th.	(20)	
40.	Central African Republic	240 th.		
41.	Malagasy Republic*	230 th.	(20)	
42.	Kenya	220 th.		
43.	Botswana	220 th.		
44.	France	210 th.		
45.	Thailand	200 th.		
46.	Spain	200 th.		15
47.	Cameroon	180 th.		
48.	Sweden	170 th.		
49.	Iraq	170 th.		
50.	Morocco*	160 th.	(20)	
51.	Paraguay	160 th.		
52.	Rhodesia	150 th.		
53.	Japan*	140 th.	(15)	
54.	Congo (Brazzaville)	130 th.		
55.	Finland*	130 th.	(15)	
56.	Malaysia	130 th.		
57.	Vietnam	127 th.		
58.	Norway*	125 th.	(15)	10
59.	Ivory Coast	125 th.		
60.	Poland	120 th.		
61.	Italy	120 th.		
62.	Philippines	120 th.		
63.	Yemen (Aden)*	110 th.	(15)	

*A bonus weight value of 5 points is added for nations occupying crucial strategic locations on sea lanes.

47

Country	Square Miles	Perceived Power Weight
64. Ecuador	110 th.	
65. Upper Volta	110 th.	
66. New Zealand	100 th.	
67. Gabon	100 th.	
68. Yugoslavia	100 th.	(10)
69. West Germany (FRG)	100 th.	
70. Guinea	95 th.	
71. United Kingdom*	94 th.	(15)

*A bonus weight value of 5 points is added for nations occupying crucial strategic locations on sea lanes.

If we add the appropriate weights for the largest territorial holdings to the 42 nations with the largest populations, we have a ranklist providing weights for the term "C" in the perceived power formula. Countries weighted as being in the higher three groups in extent of area, that is, with more than 500,000 square miles, are added to our consolidated list even if their population size (under 15,000,000) does not qualify them for it. There are many refinements in the power equation to be made for each country. On the basis of particular economic, military, and political factors, some nations must be designated as powerful in a special sense because of those factors even though both their population and territory are small. Singapore and Israel are examples. If countries later come into consideration because of other strengths, their total power rating will also be increased on the basis of the weight values given them for territorial extent, even though the territorial factor alone does not qualify for the consolidated list of critical mass. The procedure we have followed generally gives a little more importance to people than to territory, since populous countries of an adequate size can exploit economic resources, mobilize armies, and bring their influence to bear on others.

The ranklist compiled on the basis of critical mass contains only four countries (Australia, Mongolia, Libya, and Saudi Arabia) included purely because of the size of their territories as distinct from those with large populations. Since all four happen to be nations with enormous deserts and relatively small populations, they do not alter the character of the total 46-nation ranklist very much.

Consolidated Ranklist: Critical Mass (Population and Territory)

Country	Perceived Power Weight
1. USSR	100
2. United States	100
3. China (PRC)	100
4. India	90
5. Brazil	85
6. Indonesia	80
7. Canada	70
8. Mexico	70
9. Argentina	65
10. Iran	60
11. Japan	60
12. Nigeria	60
13. Pakistan	60
14. Zaire	55
15. United Kingdom	55
16. France	55
17. Turkey	55
18. Egypt	55
19. West Germany (FRG)	50
20. Italy	50
21. Burma	50
22. South Africa	50
23. Ethiopia	45
24. Thailand	45
25. Spain	45
26. Sudan	40
27. Algeria	40
28. Australia	40
29. Colombia	40
30. Philippines	40
31. Vietnam	40
32. Bangladesh	40
33. Poland	35

Country	Perceived Power Weight
34. Afghanistan	30
35. Morocco	30
36. Yugoslavia	30
37. South Korea	30
38. Tanzania	30
39. Peru	30
40. Libya	30
41. Saudi Arabia	30
42. Mongolia	30
43. Rumania	20
44. East Germany (GDR)	10
45. North Korea	10
46. China/Taiwan	10
Total	**2,245**

The consideration of population and territory by themselves as basic factors constituting critical mass in the international arena ends up with countries at the top of the list which are *prima facie* of consequence or certainly of so much potential consequence that any assessment of the international balance of power must pay special attention to them.

This means that the 46 major countries in the world as calculated purely on the basis of people and possession of land are those which most observers of international events would call to mind. It is still a crude list but one that we can work with and modify with confidence that we are talking about actual perceptions of power. As anyone would expect, the big three are China, the USSR, and the United States. This consolidated critical mass ranklist needs much refinement but even at this stage it conforms to most subjective judgments of conditions in the world today.

It may be useful now to note how these major nations are distributed among the politectonic zones of the globe. They provide the foundation, though not the exclusive subject, of our ongoing assessment. The weights that we have assigned constitute units of perceived power, a kind of abstract measure of the international importance of each zone, judged at this point in our calculation only by the simple criteria of size, strategic location, and population of leading nations. Three Communist countries are difficult to assign with respect to politectonic zones, and this fact is indicated by footnotes.

Politectonic Zones: Critical Mass of Major Nations

	Country	Critical Mass	Total of Perceived Power Weights
I	United States	100	
	Canada	70	240
	Mexico	70	
II	USSR	100	
	Poland	35	
	Mongolia	30	195
	Rumania	20	
	East Germany (GDR)	10	
III	China (PRC)	100	
	Vietnam*	40	150*
	North Korea*	10	
IV	France	55	
	United Kingdom	55	
	West Germany (FRG)	50	285**
	Italy	50	
	Spain	45	
	Yugoslavia**	30	
V	Iran	60	
	Turkey	55	
	Egypt	55	
	Sudan	40	340
	Algeria	40	
	Morocco	30	
	Libya	30	
	Saudi Arabia	30	
VI	India	90	
	Pakistan	60	220
	Bangladesh	40	
	Afghanistan	30	
VII	Indonesia	80	
	Burma	50	215
	Thailand	45	
	Philippines	40	

	Country	Critical Mass	Total of Perceived Power Weights
VIII	Japan	60	100
	South Korea	30	
	China/Taiwan	10	
IX	Brazil	85	220
	Argentina	65	
	Colombia	40	
	Peru	30	
X	Nigeria	60	240
	Zaire	55	
	South Africa	50	
	Ethiopia	45	
	Tanzania	30	
XI	Australia	40	40
			Total 2,245

*Including independent Communist Vietnam and North Korea is dubious politically and strategically as distinct from geographically, but regional links have some importance.
**Including nonaligned Communist Yugoslavia is dubious strategically as distinct from geographically. Without it the value for West Europe would be 255.

It is apparent that some zones are of great potential importance because of the critical mass of the nations in them but are weakened by political separatism and fragmentation at the present time. Intra-regional conflicts in the Mideast and in Central and Southern Africa are especially damaging to regional exercise of national power and hence to world perceptions of the importance of these zones.

The nations listed are in a general sense the principal eligible players in the game of international politics. Many of them are not yet able to take a strong position standing alone and have not formed stable alliance relationships. A few others will emerge as eligible players because of economic or military strengths realized apart from size of population or territory. Some of the 46 single nations thus singled out have not been able to develop economic and military resources commensurate with their size. Our politectonic assessment is only at a first-phase plateau. More refined measurements must be introduced.

CHAPTER THREE

Measuring Economic Capabilities
$P_p = (C + E + M) \times (S + W)$

In developing a formula for measuring and comparing national power it is clear that calculations based solely on territory and people would be misleading unless adjusted to show particular economic strengths developed by the people in managing the resources of the land. In other words, the formula $P_p = C$ is too crude a measure; the equation is more useful—although still incomplete—if it reads $P_p = C + E$. What the people of a country have actually accomplished, or could presumably accomplish in short order, with their material and spiritual wealth, is a critical factor in their own and others' perceptions of their power. Economic strength is the basis on which a nation satisfies the needs of its people for goods and services, and also on which it is able to build its organized military capabilities, to manufacture arms, to supply manpower, and to provide the logistic and technical support needed by modern armies, navies, and air forces. Through investment and trade, nations help to enrich one another, and standards of living depend not only on the efficiency of national economic activity but also on access to resources and markets through international commerce. The next task in our assessment of world power is therefore to look at countries from the economic viewpoint. While here, as elsewhere, we are dealing with macrometrics designed to support general conclusions, some greater precision in quantification is possible.

The task of measurement is not easy, however, because economic strength is a multidimensional concept with many different insights into different aspects of those economic facts of life which contribute to a broad perception of overall performance. Current economic output and wealth, which are functions of both resources and the form and effectiveness of economic organization, are crucial at moments of imminent conflict or threat, because they represent an immediate ability to respond. Over a long period of time, economic potential, which is partly a function of reserve capacities, is especially critical for maintaining a high level of economic activity, as well as for supporting military strength during a long confrontation or conflict. The economic potential for military effort in war or short-of-war conflicts is also affected by the ease and efficiency with which resources and available capacity can be reallocated to different needs, such as the production of more submarines or ICBMs in place of a greater variety of passenger automobiles.

Another qualification concerning perceptions of current economic capacity is that it may depend, often precariously, on a nation's trade relations with the rest of the world, which supplies it with either raw materials or markets for goods produced. In a world where the nation-state is still the primary actor, nations which are more self-sufficient than others—especially in terms of crucial goods such as raw materials for industry and foodstuffs—are probably perceived, rightly or wrongly, to be more powerful than others with the same level of current economic capacity.

In advanced industrial societies in peacetime, however, this self-sufficiency is more a liability, a sacrifice of economic benefits, than an asset. In times when international trade flows safely, nations that control a large share of the world's trade and investment not only improve the standard of living of their own people but also are able to exercise substantial power over other nations which want goods or capital. While the self-sufficiency of the domestic economy in critical categories is an asset, so is the leverage that foreign trade and investment can give.

Finally, what may be important—economically—for one country may not be so for another. Production of cement in the poorest nations is a measure of industrial strength, but, for the developed countries, the production of other more technologically complex goods is much more advantageous. Thus the use of quantitative measures of economic capability must be tempered by an understanding of the differences between countries at different stages of economic development. In this study, indicators have been selected mainly to reflect the capability of states to exert an influence on other nations in short-of-war conflicts or confrontations.

"Command" versus "Free Enterprise" Economics

In what are usually described as free enterprise economies, the comparatively widely dispersed control over productive resources requires a system of economic signals in order to allocate these resources efficiently. These signals take the form of prices, which link supply and demand, and the resulting decentralization of economic decisions facilitates the movement of resources to more efficient producers.

Of course no free enterprise system works with complete freedom or in perfect adjustment to supply and demand. Price signals may be incorrect, reflecting special noncompetitive agreements among major producers or inopportune government intervention through taxes, government expenditures, or management of the money supply. Producer and consumer responses to price signals may be weakened by various constraints, such as the reluctance of workers to move from Massachusetts to Texas or the faulty perceptions of business management. As a result, these imperfections reduce the theoretical efficiency of the free enterprise system.

At the other end of the spectrum, a command economy has direct centralized control over all productive resources. In theory, these resources can therefore be reallocated, forcibly if necessary, to the sectors of the economy where they are most needed. Several imperfections mar the operation of such a system. First, because the command economy does not generate its own price signals, the government must devote much highly skilled managerial talent to running the economy and adjusting resource allocation to needs. Otherwise such allocation will be neither sufficient nor timely and the presumed advantage of the centralized control will not materialize.

Because in a command economy there is likely to be only small opportunity for personal gain—e.g., profits for entrepreneurs or the chance for workers to buy cars and television sets—the productivity of resource use is often low. Even though resource allocation is easier, that does not necessarily assure a larger supply of desired products, whether they be foods, industrial machines, or weapons. No valid method exists to handle the intricacies of input-output economics on a large national scale. When it is attempted, as in the USSR, conspicuous inefficiencies result. Moreover, where there is no structural relationship between managerial and worker efficiency and financial rewards, incentives to produce efficiently are consequently low.

One of the appealing features of the command economy is its presumed ability to change the structure of demand, meaning that the government can preempt resources for national needs; for example, to divert resources to produce more weapons or to develop more sophisticated military technologies in support of armed forces. In economies where capacity is limited, this power arbitrarily to divide the economic pie and thus shift resources to the military sector may be perceived as an economic strength. On the other hand, such arbitrary control does not automatically assure that the resource shift occurs effectively, or that the shifted resources actually produce the desired outputs.

A free enterprise system, on the other hand, often responds rapidly and effectively to changed national needs, as in the case of the United States in World War II. It normally is much superior in technological and managerial innovation because these give the economic product direct cost and market benefits.

It is not completely clear, on balance, which system possesses the greater overall economic advantage, for that depends very much on special features of the economy, such as resource endowment and the diffusion of technology. Most nations maintain a mixed economy, somewhere between the Soviet command model at one end of the spectrum and the U.S. model toward the other, free enterprise, end. In the following discussions of economic strength I do not explicitly introduce qualitative factors for or against the two economic models in the ranking. Certainly the U.S. free enterprise-oriented system is inextricably interrelated with the pluralistic society and political emphasis on the individual that is part of the American cultural heritage. They tend to go together. So do dictatorship and the command economy.

To the extent that one system or the other does have operating economic advantages, it should be reflected in the several economic indicators examined in the following statistics. So what is considered here are only more or less objective measures of economic capabilities; the preference of one type of economy over the other depends more on the political and social differences between the totalitarian and the pluralistic society than on pure economics.

Measurement of Economic Capability: GNP

The most comprehensive way of calculating the extent of a country's mobilized economic strength is to assess the total value of economic goods and services produced and marketed annually, that is, the gross national product (GNP). If qualified with appropriate caveats about other aspects of a nation's economic structure, particularly its natural resources, its technological skills, and its international trade, comparisons among nations which are based on GNP are extremely revealing. Furthermore, GNP is a standard of concrete measurement made familiar by repeated worldwide use in the information media. The initial economic analysis in this chapter is based on the systematic compilation of GNP data for the calendar year 1975 issued by the U.S. Government in 1976.[1] Later data cannot be systematically manipulated for comparative purposes until some time after the economic activity occurs; hence general perceptions normally lag well behind the actual event. This fact often explains anomalies in the way the world perceives certain countries whose situation is changing rapidly for better or for worse.

What quickly emerges from an examination of these data is that most of the world's activity resulting in measurable economic goods and services takes place in a relatively small number of countries. Among these, the United States is in a class altogether by itself. The 1975 GNP of the United States was $1,500 billion—or a trillion and a half of 1975 dollars.

The total value of economic goods and services in the whole world in 1975, described in U.S. 1975 dollars, was about 6,000 billion or six trillion dollars. Thus the United States alone produced and disposed of about one-fourth of the world product in 1975. It was a period of worldwide depression and inflation, so the total value is not a great deal more, and the percentage share differs very little, if 1977 GNP rates and dollar values are used.[2] For valid comparisons, the earlier figures are safer, and, in the case of many countries, all that are available. The basic pattern of economic activity in 1975 persists in general terms down into 1977.

The Soviet economy for a number of years has been operating at a level around one-half of the GNP of the United States. Thus in 1975 the

Soviet GNP was about $790 billion, or slightly more than half of the GNP of the United States. The two superpowers together thus accounted for nearly 40 percent of the world's economic output; and with Japan ($490 billion) and the Federal Republic of Germany ($425 billion), for over one-half of the global GNP. Another trillion U.S. 1975 dollars is accounted for by five other nations: France ($340 billion), the United Kingdom ($180 billion), Italy ($170 billion), Canada ($140 billion), and the People's Republic of China ($260 billion). Thus the nine nations with the largest GNPs account for two-thirds of the world's economic output. The top 46 nations ranked according to critical mass of population and territory in the preceding chapter account for 90 percent of the economic goods and services of the entire globe.

The ranking system we employ for GNP is straightforward and assigns a score or weight of one hundred for the highest ranking country, the United States, giving proportionately lesser scores to nations with smaller GNPs.[3] This preliminary ranking will be adjusted and refined after we examine additional economic details specific to each country. By including all nations with a 1975 GNP of 10 or more billion U.S. 1975 dollars, we create a ranklist of 53 nations, including most, although not all, of the countries ranking high in critical mass.

GNP for 53 Leading Countries in Billions of U.S. 1975 Dollars (Rounded)

Country	GNP 1975 (billion $U.S. rounded)	Perceived Power Weight
1. United States	1,500	100
2. USSR	790	52
3. Japan	485	32
4. FRG	420	28
5. France	340	22
6. PRC	260	17
7. United Kingdom	230	15
8. Italy	170	11
9. Canada	150	10
10. Spain	100	7
11. Brazil	90	6
12. India	80	5
13. Poland	80	5

	Country	GNP 1975 (billion $U.S. rounded)	Perceived Power Weight
14.	Australia	80	5
15.	Mexico	80	5
16.	GDR	70	5
17.	Netherlands	70	5
18.	Sweden	70	5
19.	Czechoslovakia	55	4
20.	Iran	50	3
21.	Belgium	45	3
22.	Rumania	45	3
23.	Switzerland	45	3
24.	Argentina	40	3
25.	Yugoslavia	35	2
26.	Saudi Arabia	35	2
27.	South Africa	30	2
28.	Austria	30	2
29.	Denmark	30	2
30.	Indonesia	30	2
31.	Hungary	25	2
32.	Venezuela	25	2
33.	Nigeria	25	2
34.	Turkey	25	2
35.	Norway	25	2
36.	Bulgaria	20	1
37.	Finland	20	1
38.	South Korea	20	1
39.	Greece	20	1
40.	Iraq	15	1
41.	Philippines	15	1
42.	China/Taiwan	15	1
43.	Algeria	15	1
44.	Thailand	15	1
45.	Colombia	15	1
46.	Libya	10	1
47.	New Zealand	10	1
48.	Peru	10	1
49.	Israel	10	1
50.	Portugal	10	1
51.	Kuwait	10	1
52.	Egypt	10	1
53.	Pakistan	10	1

Special Economic Strengths and Weaknesses

As an aggregate measure, GNP necessarily conceals many special features in an economy. Some of these strengths and weaknesses have a substantial impact on the perceived image of national power in international relations. For this reason, for certain countries, we need to adjust the rankings above, based solely on GNP.

We have selected five broad factors which can be used to modify or adjust the GNP-based rankings: energy, minerals, industrial strength, agriculture, and foreign economic relations. Because perceived power is a relative concept by which nations compare themselves, or are compared, to other nations, these special characteristics are for the most part measured relative to an international standard of economic performance.

Each country is assigned an additional value for each of these supplemental measures of economic strength, with a possible additional total of 100 weight units, or 20 for each special economic strength. These values may be viewed as bonus economic weights above and beyond GNP. In a few cases of otherwise economically powerful nations, specific weaknesses are so apparent that a negative value must be taken into account—by subtracting units of power weights from the overall economic total. GNP is still perceived as the major determinant of economic strength, but its value may be increased or decreased in proportion to such a special economic strength or weakness.

Energy

Clearly, energy is one of the most vital components of economic power, particularly in highly industrialized countries. Current energy consumption is, of course, closely correlated with the level of GNP, and, to some extent, has already been measured. But one special aspect of energy can easily and profoundly affect both present and potential economic and military power; it is energy adequacy or—in the negative case—dependency.

As experience during the 1973-1974 OPEC oil embargo demonstrated, the need to rely on foreign suppliers of energy may seriously constrain economic activity in times of shortages. Countries which must import large quantities of energy have a more precarious economic base than ones which rely primarily on domestic sources. Conversely, countries producing a surplus of energy, which they export, have under such conditions leverage over some other nations. We recognize this first special feature of energy by assigning bonus weight units, or subtracting them, to reflect in a general way the volume of current national consumption that must be imported or is exported, on a net basis. We focus on oil because it has been highly publicized as a crucial natural resource since the 1973 embargo and because it impinges on the consumer as well as on the industrial producer very directly.[4] It is also a major problem for the United States, which is one of the world's largest producers but is alone among them in nonetheless requiring massive oil imports to meet its economic needs.

World Crude Oil Production in 1975*

(million barrels daily)

	Production	Major Surplus	Consumption	Major Dependency
USSR	9.6	x	7.5	
United States	8.4		16.3	x
Saudi Arabia	7.1	x		
Iran	5.4	x		
Venezuela	2.4	x		
Iraq	2.3	x		
Kuwait	2.1	x		
Nigeria	1.8	x		
United Arab Emirates	1.7	x		
Canada	1.5		1.8	
Libya	1.5	x		
PRC	1.3		1.1	
Indonesia	1.3			
Japan	y		4.9	x
FRG	y		2.7	x
France	y		2.2	x
United Kingdom	y		1.9	x
Italy	y		1.9	x

*Handbook of Economic Statistics 1976, DOCEX, Library of Congress, Washington, D.C., and BP Statistical Review of the World Oil Industry 1975, British Petroleum Company, Ltd., London, England.

y = negligible production

This energy sufficiency information based on oil production, consumption, and export/import data must be corrected by some allowance for supplies of the other fossil fuel, coal, which has been much less exported and hence less noted as a source of energy, but which is still widely used and essential in most modern economies.

The principal coal producers, along with the three main coal importers, are:

Hard Coal

(million metric tons)

Major Producing Countries	1975 Production	
1. United States	570	
2. USSR	485	
3. PRC	430	
4. Poland	170	
5. United Kingdom	130	
6. FRG	95	
7. India	95	
8. South Africa	70	
9. Australia	65	
Major Importing Countries	*1975 Imports*	*Major Dependency*
10. Japan	62	x
11. France	17	
12. Italy	12	

All coal production figures are from *Handbook of Economic Statistics 1976,* DOCEX, Library of Congress, Washington, D.C. Export/import figures are from the U.S. Department of the Interior, *International Coal Trade,* Vol. 45, No. 8, August 1976.

There is one more element in energy production which looms large in the future and even larger in the public perception of its importance, and that is nuclear energy. Here the picture is straightforward. The industry is in its infancy and the United States is far in the lead. At present, nuclear energy accounts for something on the order of 1 to 2 percent of international energy production. There are approximately 175 nuclear power reactors now operating worldwide, with about as many more under construction or planned.[5]

Major Nations With Nuclear Power Reactors (1976)

Countries	Thousand Megawatts of Power	Reactors
1. United States	45.4	60
2. United Kingdom	10.5	33
3. USSR	7.3	20
4. Japan	7.1	10
5. FRG	6.2	7
6. Canada	3.3	7
7. Sweden	3.2	5
8. France	2.9	10
9. Belgium	1.7	3
10. Switzerland	1.0	3

While cost factors and construction delays due to environmental concerns in some nations, especially the United States, have kept the world nuclear energy component a minor factor, the dynamics of the situation and the sheer fascination of the public with nuclear energy suggest that some bonus economic weights must be added to a calculation of economic strength in the energy field to account for technological progress in constructing nuclear reactors.

From all of these data it is possible to construct a table of bonuses and minuses for general perceived power weights in the energy field. It obviously hinges mainly on oil availability but is modified in some cases by possession of coal and nuclear reactors.

Energy

Country	Oil	Major Import Dependency	Coal	Major Import Dependency	Nuclear	Perceived Power Weights
1. USSR	10		5		2	17
2. United States	8	−5	5		5	13
3. Saudi Arabia	7					7
4. PRC	1		4			5
5. Iran	5					5
6. Canada	2				1	3
7. Kuwait	2					2
8. United Arab Emirates	2					2
9. Iraq	2					2
10. Venezuela	2					2
11. Nigeria	2					2
12. Libya	2					2
13. Poland			2			2
14. Indonesia	1					1
15. FRG		−2	1		2	1
16. United Kingdom		−2	1		2	1
17. India			1			1
18. South Africa			1			1
19. Australia			1			1
20. Sweden					1	1
21. Belgium					1	1
22. France		−2			1	−1
23. Italy		−2				−2
24. Japan		−5		−1	2	−4

Critical Non-fuel Minerals

Some non-fuel minerals are in short supply to meet the needs of advanced industrial technology. Here the relevant measure is not total production so much as the adequacy of a nation's production for its domestic uses. The high consumption of these minerals is already in part measured by the level of GNP and the degree of industrial capacity. Heavy reliance on foreign sources is commonly perceived as a disadvantage to a nation. On the other hand, if it possesses or has control over

Iron Ore*

(million metric tons rounded)
1975

Countries	Production	Perceived Power Weight	Exports	Perceived Power Weight	Imports	Major Import Dependency	Net Perceived Power Weight
1. USSR	233	10	43	2			12
2. PRC	109	5					5
3. Australia	99	4	80	4			8
4. United States	81	4			49		2
5. Japan					131	−2	−6
6. FRG					44	−6	−2
						−2	

*Handbook of Economic Statistics, 1976, op. cit. Export/import figures are from U.N. Monthly Bulletin of Statistics, August, 1976, pp. 42-43.

critical minerals which other nations want to draw upon, then it will derive economic leverage from this situation.

Five non-fuel minerals are especially critical in modern industry: *iron ore, copper, bauxite, chromium,* and *uranium.* We treat iron ore as of special weight because its use is basic and widespread, particularly in heavy industry and military weapons manufacture. As with energy, we calculate the bonus effects of production plus, in a few cases, net exports of iron ore from a country, and treat substantial imports as negative values because of the dependency they reflect. Countries are assigned economic bonus or negative adjustment factors according to their deviation from the world average.

The other four minerals—although they are all used in smaller quantities, are scattered among different regions, and, in most cases, could in emergencies, given time, be recycled or replaced with substitutes—are essential for some specialized types of manufacturing. Copper conductors, aluminum, and chrome alloys are integral to many light and heavy industries; uranium is increasingly meaningful as the world thinks of turning to nuclear reactors for its energy. As with iron ore, we calculate net exports and treat imports as negative factors, assigning weights based on the primacy of iron ore with the other four minerals collectively weighted as a little less than equal in value (12 versus 8) with iron ore.

Refined Copper*

(million metric tons rounded)
1975

Countries	Production	Exports	Imports	Net Perceived Power Weights
1. United States	1.6			2
2. USSR	1.3			2
3. Japan	0.8		0.2	1
4. Zambia	0.6	0.6		2
5. Chile	0.5	0.5		2
6. Canada	0.5	0.3		1
7. United Kingdom			0.4	−1
8. France			0.4	−1
9. Italy			0.3	−1

Handbook of Economic Statistics, 1976, op. cit. Export/import figures are from World Bureau of Metal Statistics, Birmingham, England, 1976.

Bauxite*

(million metric tons rounded)
1975

Countries	Production	Perceived Power Weights
1. Australia	20.3	2
2. Jamaica	12.7	2
3. Guinea	7.1	2
4. USSR	6.6	1
5. Surinam	5.9	1
6. Guyana	2.4	1

*Handbook of Economic Statistics, 1976, op. cit.

Chromite*

(million metric tons rounded)
1975

Countries	Production	Perceived Power Weights
1. USSR	3.5	2
2. South Africa	.8	1
3. Albania	.7	1
4. Turkey	.3	1
5. Rhodesia	.3	1

* Handbook of Economic Statistics, 1976, op. cit.

Uranium*

(thousands of tons of U_3O_8)
1975

Countries**	Production	Perceived Power Weights
1. United States	11.6	2
2. Canada	4.6	1
3. South Africa***	3.2	1
4. France	2.2	1

*Statistics from Energy Research and Development Administration.
**Soviet uranium production, which probably includes the production of several East European Communist states, is not reported outside of the USSR but is estimated to be perhaps one-half to two-thirds of U.S. production. Because of this uncertainty, no bonus value is added, although a weight of one bonus would probably be due if the USSR were not so secretive about its resources.
***Includes production figures for the Territory of South-West Africa (Namibia).

The total values for perceived power weights of nations with respect to critical minerals add up as follows:

Critical Minerals

1975

Countries	*Iron Ore*	*Copper*	*Bauxite*	*Chromite*	*Uranium*	*TOTAL*
		Perceived Power Weights				
1. USSR	12	2	1	2		17
2. Australia	8		2			10
3. United States	2	2			2	6
4. PRC	5					5
5. South Africa				1	1	2
6. Canada		1			1	2
7. Jamaica			2			2
8. Guinea			2			2
9. Zambia		2				2
10. Chile		2				2
11. Rhodesia				1		1
12. Turkey				1		1
13. Albania				1		1
14. Guyana			1			1
15. Surinam			1			1
16. France		−1			1	0
17. United Kingdom		−1				−1
18. Italy		−1				−1
19. FRG	−2					−2
20. Japan	−6	1				−5

Industry

Industrial might is closely associated with a nation's economic capability, since it represents that nation's ability to fabricate the basic materials of heavy manufacturing, machine tools, many consumer goods, and, of course, military hardware. For the past century the predominant place in industry has been held by steel. It goes into almost everything that builds manufacturing capability. Soviet leaders have always favored, while sometimes complaining about "steel-eaters," the economic and military weapons planners who demand more and more steel. In fact, the Soviets are wasting steel and at the same time forced to import high-quality steels. Developing nations are always thrilled with their first steel plant. The gross magnitude of national steel production is one of the most appropriate measurements of the strength of an industrial nation.[6]

This is especially true of all the nations which have not yet reached the advanced state of the economy of the United States, which has been called a "post-industrial" society because its plant is so large that it can satisfy industrial needs easily, and a large proportion of economic activity is centered in the service industries, rather than in manufacturing. Self-sufficiency in steel was in a sense assessed earlier by the variable dealing with a nation's dependency on importing iron ore for its supply of this critical mineral. In any case, it is their level of steel production which other nations consider in assessing the industrial might of adversaries or allies, particularly because of its importance in manufacturing heavy military weapons and equipment.

An additional metal industry can be used to measure economic capability because it is widely used in light industry and consumers' equipment manufacturing: aluminum. Here, too, the gross magnitude of national production is a good index of performance, and self-sufficiency has already in a sense been assessed by looking at the relatively few nations producing bauxite on a large scale. Treating steel as central because it is a crucial commodity in military weapons, additional bonus weights are assigned on a basis which sets 15 as a maximum allowance for steel production and 5 as a maximum allowance for aluminum manufacturing.

Steel Production*

(million metric tons rounded)
1975

Countries	Production	Perceived Power Weights
1. USSR	141	15
2. United States	105	10
3. Japan	102	10
4. FRG	40	4
5. PRC	26	3
6. France	21	2
7. Italy	21	2
8. United Kingdom	20	2

Handbook of Economic Statistics, 1976, op. cit.

Aluminum Production*

(million metric tons rounded)
1975

Countries	Production	Perceived Power Weights
1. United States	3.5	5
2. USSR	2.4	3
3. Japan	1.0	2
4. Canada	0.8	1
5. FRG	0.7	1

Handbook of Economic Statistics, 1976, op. cit.

Foods

The 1970s have repeatedly demonstrated that agricultural capacity may in the future be one of the most critical components of economic power. Nations that must import food suffer from the uncertainty of dealing on sometimes tight international markets, may have to endure domestic disruptions if food is inadequate, and, in any case, use valuable foreign reserves that could otherwise purchase minerals, machines, technology, and weapons. On the other hand, nations which produce a surplus of food commodities are insulated from the vagaries of the climate and the international market (though not from their own farm lobbies), and also possess potential bargaining power in international relations.

Although the effects of a strong or weak agriculture may be quite marked, objective and concise measurement of agricultural potential and capacity is not easy. Consideration of resources alone, such as arable land, is inadequate because the productivity of land varies so widely. For example, rice yields in Asia may be several times the yields in Africa. Land may be the fundamental factor of agricultural production, but its usefulness depends heavily on the corresponding climate, the amount of labor and machinery available to till it, and the level of chemical and biological technology applied to agricultural production. Moreover, the arable land may be used for industrial agricultural crops rather than for food production.

Consideration of output alone, such as cereals production, is also inadequate because not all cereals are used directly for human consumption. For example, in the United States, over 50 percent of total cereal production is used for animals, most of which in turn are used for food. This agriculture-food pattern is inherently a less efficient producer of calories than a more primitive economic pattern of behavior in which cereal plants are consumed directly. To complicate matters, some countries—such as Argentina and Australia—have a relatively low cereals production, yet raise large quantities of beef by using natural grasslands, which otherwise would be unproductive. A measurement based on cereals alone might understate the agricultural strength of these countries.

Furthermore, governments are usually heavily involved in the agricultural sector in most countries. Their intervention may cause distortions, such as suppressing possible agricultural production, as was done in the United States for many years in order to maintain higher prices for the benefit of farmers. A measure based solely on current output would in this case understate real U.S. capacity.

Finally, any measures of agricultural production must be considered relative to a country's population. More heavily populated countries require more agricultural production, and greater density usually means there is more manpower for agriculture, which normally raises yields. The case of the People's Republic of China is relevant. Most of the GNP of the PRC is based on agriculture, and about 80 percent of the vast Chinese population lives in rural areas and subsists mainly by agricultural labor. The magnitude of this effort nevertheless produces no food surplus and the country, despite its size, is in no sense economically strong because of this need to employ most of its labor force in feeding the population at a mere subsistence level.

Unfortunately, agricultural production data expressed in some common denominator such as calories are not available, so we fall back on comparing production in metric tons. Production of the three major grains, wheat, rice, and corn, is examined for the main agricultural nations. Obviously this procedure ignores other small grains, root crops such as potatoes, and the fact that much corn, especially, is used for animal rather than human food. We also consider net exports of the major cereals, but for lack of comparative data ignore the fact that some grains are traded in the form of meat; a country's exports of beef may be considered as exports of the corn fed to the beef, but this is a refinement we have not introduced in our macrometrics.

To provide some objective basis for perceptions of strength deriving from the capability to produce foods, we quantify three variable agricultural characteristics. The first is total hectares of arable land. Countries with more arable land on the whole strike observers as possessing greater potential agricultural power, although this way of measuring is very crude.

Second, we list production and calculate the productivity of agricultural effort by noting the total tons of major cereals produced and then dividing the sum by the total hectares used to produce this tonnage. These data represent a crude measure of agricultural productivity, slightly more refined than the gross production figures alone. Greater yields per hectare imply the country is more richly endowed and/or has devoted greater resources, both physical and technological, to agricultural production. Therefore, these countries probably have a greater perceived power as a result of this special economic strength.

Third, and most important in the international context, we compare net exports and imports, which are in effect negative exports. Countries that export cereals possess economic advantages stemming from a high level of agricultural output, while countries that import cereals have weak economies because in comparison they lack the leverage in international affairs that surplus foods provide in a frequently hungry world. The bonus weights for perceived power or negative weights for dependency are mainly assigned on the basis of this export-import data.

The importance of what has been called "agripower" was highlighted in world perceptions as a result of the "great grain robbery" of 1972 whereby the USSR offset its own very bad harvests by purchasing millions of tons of American grain at prices that were both at bargain levels and subsidized by the U.S. taxpayers by a system set up in a period of persistent wheat and corn surpluses. Clearly one of the strongest bargaining chips the United States has for strengthening its alliances is its abundance of food, a key staple in international trade in most recent years and likely to become more so in view of the burden of world population growth on slower growing food production capacity.

It has been observed that Marx was a "city boy," overstressing industry. In any event, the USSR has been unsuccessful, with its system of nearly incentiveless collective farms, in insuring an adequate food grain supply to feed the population and at the same time move toward the more costly system of animal husbandry that would permit the standard of Soviet living to rise to support a nation of meat-eaters, as the people want and the Soviet government repeatedly promises. The PRC

Foods*

1975

Countries	Wheat				Corn				Rice				Net Perceived Power Weights
	Hectares** Cultivated (millions rounded)	Production (million metric tons rounded)	Productivity (yield/hectare)	Net Exports/Imports (million metric tons rounded)	Hectares* Cultivated (millions rounded)	Production (million metric tons rounded)	Productivity (yield/hectare)	Net Exports/Imports (million metric tons rounded)	Hectares* Cultivated (millions rounded)	Production (million metric tons rounded)	Productivity (yield/hectare)	Net Exports/Imports (million metric tons rounded)	
1. United States	28	58	2	32	27	146	5.4	43	1	6	5.1	1.9	20
2. Canada	9	17	1.7	12	6	4	5.7						3
3. France	39	15	3.8	8.5	1.9	8	4.7	2.1					3
4. Australia	8	12	1.4	9									2
5. Argentina	5.2	8	1.6	4	2.8	6	2	2					2
6. South Africa					4.5	8	1.8	1.8					1
7. Thailand									8	15	1.7	1.3	0
8. Japan									3	15	5.5		0
9. Burma									5	9	1.8		0
10. Bangladesh									10	20	1.9	-0.4	0
11. Indonesia									9	22	2.5	-0.7	0
12. PRC	27	38	1.4	-2.4	14	32	2.2		34	122	3.5	1.2	-1
13. Brazil		9		-3.6	11	17	1.5	2.2	6	8	1.3		-1
14. Mexico					8	9	1.1	-1.7					-1
15. Italy	3.5	9	2.7	-1.3	9	5	5.9						-1
16. India	18	24	1.3	-6.8					38	69	1.6		-2
17. USSR	62	66	1.0	-10	3	7	2.7	-12				-1.1	-6

*All figures provided by the U.S. Department of Agriculture, Foreign Agricultural Service, July 1, 1976.

**One hectare is equal to 2.47 acres.

and India, which between them have approximately 40 percent of the world population, are able to feed themselves only in good harvest years. If recent trends continue, the United States may be the only major food exporter in the years ahead. It stands out far above the rest now.

Trade

Domestic economic power in our day is inextricably imbedded in an international context, and must be so evaluated. To some extent, we have already taken foreign economic relations into account, in the way we have dealt with energy dependency, critical mineral resources, and agricultural production. But because of steadily growing interdependency among national economies, every nation must factor into its perception of its own comparative economic capability some index which reflects overall strengths stemming from national participation in the world economy.

Foreign trade is a good indicator of power or leverage exercised in international economic relations. Leverage derives from domination of world trade in certain regions or in certain commodities, mainly through exporting sought-after goods and services; in some cases an essential bulk importer gets some leverage over its trading partners by providing a fundamental market. For example, an active trading nation like Japan participates in a wide array of markets across the globe and benefits from a remarkably extensive penetration in the business activities of foreigners. It is also a crucial market for many products it imports from other nations. If any country is the major supplier of some vital commodity to another, the former has economic leverage over the latter; alternatively, if a country is the major purchaser of another's primary export, it, too, has a certain kind of leverage.

Perceptions of nations as major traders in the world economy contribute to an image of power that connotes not only economic productivity but also the ability to maintain access to resources and marketplaces and lanes of commerce around the globe. The trade variable thus crudely represents a nation's influence as a supplier or user of the world's valued goods and services. Nations with a larger share of world trade are accordingly commonly perceived to have greater power in the world economy. A weighted ranklist follows showing the total trade turnover (exports plus imports) for the 30 countries which in 1975 conducted more than $12 billion U.S. dollars worth of trade.

World Trade 1975

(total: 1,590,000 billions)
All figures in billions
of dollars rounded

	Country	Exports	Imports	Total Trade	% World Trade	Perceived Power Weight
1.	United States	107	96	203	12.7	20
2.	FRG	92	75	167	10.4	16
3.	Japan	56	58	114	7.1	11
4.	France	52	54	106	6.6	10
5.	United Kingdom	44	53	97	5.9	9
6.	Italy	35	38	73	4.5	7
7.	USSR	33	37	70	4.4	7
8.	Netherlands	35	35	70	4.4	7
9.	Canada	34	32	66	4.1	7
10.	Belgium*	29	31	60	3.8	6
11.	Sweden	17	18	35	2.2	4
12.	Saudi Arabia	28	7	35	2.2	4
13.	Iran	20	11	31	1.9	4
14.	Switzerland	13	13	26	1.6	3
15.	Spain	8	16	24	1.5	2
16.	Poland	13	10	23	1.5	2
17.	Brazil	9	13	22	1.4	2
18.	Australia	11	10	21	1.3	2
19.	GDR	11	10	21	1.3	2
20.	Denmark	9	10	19	1.2	2
21.	Czechoslovakia	8	9	17	1.1	2
22.	Norway	7	10	17	1.1	2
23.	Austria	8	9	17	1.1	2
24.	Venezuela	10	6	16	1.0	2
25.	Nigeria	8	6	14	.9	1
26.	Singapore	5	8	13	.8	1
27.	Hungary	6	7	13	.8	1
28.	Finland	8	5	13	.8	1
29.	South Africa	5	8	13	.8	1
30.	South Korea	5	7	12	.75	1
31.	Indonesia	7	5	12	.75	1
32.	Yugoslavia	4	8	12	.75	1
33.	China/Taiwan	5	6	11	.7	1
34.	Iraq	8	3	11	.7	1
35.	Kuwait	9	2	11	.7	1

Sources: *UN Monthly Bulletin of Statistics,* August 1976; *International Financial Statistics,* Vol. xxx, No. 1 (Washington, D.C.: IMF, January 1977).
*Includes Luxembourg.

To recapitulate our findings, we can construct a consolidated ranklist weighted for GNP and for the five special economic factors examined in this chapter. The 63 nations thus ranked are as follows:

Economic Capability: Summary

Country	GNP (100)	Energy (20)	Minerals (20)	Industry (20)	Food (20)	Trade (20)	TOTAL
1. United States	100	13	6	15	20	20	174
2. USSR	52	17	17	18	-6	7	105
3. FRG	28	1	-2	5		16	48
4. Japan	32	-4	-5	12		11	46
5. France	22	-1		2	3	10	36
6. PRC	17	5	5	3	-1		29
7. Canada	10	3	2	1	3	7	26
8. UK	15	1	-1	2		9	26
9. Australia	5	1	10		2	2	20
10. Italy	11	-2	-1	2	-1	7	16
11. Saudi Arabia	2	7				4	13
12. Netherlands	5					7	12
13. Iran	3	5				4	12
14. Sweden	5	1				4	10
15. Belgium	3	1				6	10
16. Spain	7					2	9
17. Poland	5	2				2	9
18. South Africa	2	1	2		1	1	7
19. Brazil	6				-1	2	7
20. GDR	5					2	7
21. Czechoslovakia	4					2	6
22. Switzerland	3					3	6
23. Venezuela	2	2				2	6
24. Argentina	3				2		5
25. Nigeria	2	2				1	5
26. India	5	1			-2		4
27. Mexico	5				-1		4
28. Austria	2					2	4
29. Denmark	2					2	4
30. Indonesia	2	1				1	4
31. Norway	2					2	4
32. Iraq	1	2				1	4
33. Kuwait	1	2				1	4

Country	GNP (100)	Energy (20)	Minerals (20)	Industry (20)	Food (20)	Trade (20)	TOTAL
34. Rumania	3						3
35. Yugoslavia	2					1	3
36. Hungary	2					1	3
37. Turkey	2		1				3
38. Libya	1	2					3
39. Finland	1					1	2
40. South Korea	1					1	2
41. China/Taiwan	1					1	2
42. United Arab Emirates		2					2
43. Zambia			2				2
44. Chile			2				2
45. Jamaica			2				2
46. Guinea			2				2
47. Philippines	1						1
48. Bulgaria	1						1
49. Greece	1						1
50. Algeria	1						1
51. Thailand	1						1
52. Colombia	1						1
53. New Zealand	1						1
54. Peru	1						1
55. Israel	1						1
56. Portugal	1						1
57. Egypt	1						1
58. Pakistan	1						1
59. Surinam			1				1
60. Albania			1				1
61. Rhodesia			1				1
62. Singapore						1	1
63. Guyana			1				1

At this point we can construct a table of the countries which register on our macrometric scale of international perceptions of power as a result not only of their critical mass of population and territory but also of their economic capability.

Consolidated Ranklist:
Critical Mass and Economic Capability

Country	Critical Mass	Economic Weight	TOTAL
1. United States	100	174	274
2. USSR	100	105	205
3. PRC	100	29	129
4. Japan	60	46	106
5. FRG	50	48	98
6. Canada	70	26	96
7. India	90	4	94
8. Brazil	85	7	92
9. France	55	36	91
10. Indonesia	80	4	84
11. United Kingdom	55	26	81
12. Mexico	70	4	74
13. Iran	60	12	72
14. Argentina	65	5	70
15. Italy	50	16	66
16. Nigeria	60	5	65
17. Pakistan	60	1	61
18. Australia	40	20	60
19. Turkey	55	3	58
20. South Africa	50	7	57
21. Egypt	55	1	56
22. Zaire	55		55
23. Spain	45	9	54
24. Burma	50		50
25. Thailand	45	1	46
26. Ethiopia	45		45
27. Poland	35	9	44
28. Saudi Arabia	30	13	43
29. Philippines	40	1	41
30. Algeria	40	1	41
31. Colombia	40	1	41
32. Sudan	40		40
33. Vietnam	40		40

Country	Critical Mass	Economic Weight	TOTAL
34. Bangladesh	40		40
35. Yugoslavia	30	3	33
36. Libya	30	3	33
37. South Korea	30	2	32
38. Peru	30	1	31
39. Afghanistan	30		30
40. Morocco	30		30
41. Tanzania	30		30
42. Mongolia	30		30
43. Venezuela	20*	6	26
44. Sweden	15*	10	25
45. Rumania	20	3	23
46. Zambia	20*	2	22
47. Chile	20*	2	22
48. Norway	15*	4	19
49. Iraq	15*	4	19
50. GDR	10	7	17
51. Finland	15*	2	17
52. Rhodesia	15*	1	16
53. China/Taiwan	10	2	12
54. Netherlands		12	12
55. Guinea	10*	2	12
56. New Zealand	10*	1	11
57. North Korea	10		10
58. Belgium		10	10
59. Czechoslovakia		6	6
60. Switzerland		6	6
61. Austria		4	4
62. Denmark		4	4
63. Kuwait		4	4
64. Hungary		3	3
65. United Arab Emirates		2	2
66. Jamaica		2	2
67. Bulgaria		1	1
68. Greece		1	1
69. Israel		1	1
70. Portugal		1	1
71. Surinam		1	1
72. Albania		1	1
73. Singapore		1	1
74. Guyana		1	1

*These perceived power weights for critical mass are added here in the case of countries with substantial territory but comparatively small populations. (See p. 48.)

Critical Mass and Economic Capability:
Larger Nations in Politectonic Zones

	Country	Perceived Power Weight	Total Weights
I	United States	274	
	Canada	96	444
	Mexico	74	
II	USSR	205	205
III	PRC	129	129
IV	West Germany (FRG)	98	
	France	91	
	United Kingdom	81	390
	Italy	66	
	Spain	54	
V	Iran	72	
	Turkey	58	186
	Egypt	56	
VI	India	94	155
	Pakistan	61	
VII	Indonesia	84	84
VIII	Japan	106	106
IX	Brazil	92	162
	Argentina	70	
X	Nigeria	65	
	South Africa	57	177
	Zaire	55	
XI	Australia	60	60

We now have a consolidated ranklist at the top of which are 23 nations with combined perceived power weights of more than 50. These nations clearly appear to be leading actors on the international scene. If we arrange these countries according to the politectonic zones to which they belong, they already at this stage of our analysis of the world distribution of power suggest some broad observations: (a) the United States is stronger than the USSR and towers above the others over the whole globe; (b) North America is naturally a rich and powerful zone because it has three large nations in it; (c) West Europe is an extremely valuable piece of real estate, mainly because of the industrial technology and skills of the several major countries there; (d) the USSR alone looms large in comparison with every other zone except North America and West Europe; and (e) the People's Republic of China, despite its vast population, is a secondary power more on the order of magnitude of Japan and West Germany than a true equal of the United States and the Soviet Union. If perceptions of world power derived exclusively from population, territory, and economic capability, the distribution of lasting elements of power around the globe would be accurately reflected in the table below; in fact, of course, military capability, strategic purpose, and political skill in mobilizing national will affect power perceptions substantially, as subsequent chapters will demonstrate.

CHAPTER FOUR

Military Capability:
The Strategic Force Balance
$P_p = (C + E + M) \times (S + W)$

The ultimate sanction in disputes between nations is the use of military force. As Clausewitz said, "War is a mere continuation of policy by other means; . . . an act of violence intended to compel our opponent to fulfill our will" by "the utmost use of force."[1]

Conflicts among nations usually start with political arguments and diplomatic pressures and proceed through the offering or withholding of increasingly important economic benefits. If either side considers that the conflict affects its vital interests, it can threaten to go to war and, in the end, actually call upon its military forces in a violent act of persuasion. At the point when the use of armed force is threatened, mobilized military capabilities become all-important, whether the readiness of the superior force settles the issue without actual fighting, or, if war actually breaks out, the arbitration takes place on the battlefield. In any calculation of perceived power it is essential, then, to expand our formula for calculating national power to include military capability: $P_p = C + E + M$.

The most powerful weapons in the long history of war are universally considered to be nuclear, even though, except for Hiroshima and Nagasaki, atomic weapons remain untested under battle conditions. The overwhelming preponderance of Soviet and U.S. strategic nuclear strength is the dominant fact of international life. These two powers can literally extinguish the life of most other nations in a few moments, devastating it beyond recovery. Other nuclear powers pale into insignificance by comparison, but there is a certain aura of membership in the "nuclear club" that sets off the United Kingdom, France, China (PRC), and now possibly India from the rest. Even those nations like Japan, Sweden, Argentina, South Africa, Israel, and China/Taiwan, which are widely perceived to have the technological capability to build nuclear weapons, enjoy among their neighbors a certain marginal advantage of respect, or fear.

Nuclear weapons are so destructive that their capacity to deter other nations is their greatest military benefit. Except in an extremity hard to imagine (or in the event of unauthorized use), the United States and the USSR presently deter each other from nuclear war and seem likely to do so in the future. Obviously, either of these nuclear giants can easily deter the secondary nuclear powers from using their much more limited arsenals.

It is the implicitly threatened use of nuclear bombs or missiles—either as nuclear "blackmail" or nuclear "shield"—that brings enormous pressure to bear on international conflict situations. In a sense, the less responsible a nation's leadership, the greater the nuclear threat, for its use becomes more credible. Insofar as political leadership is moderate, and especially to the extent that it is accountable to public opinion, it can exploit nuclear capability only as a deterrent rather than as a realistic threat. Yet without this ultimate strategic weapon, no nation today can pretend to be completely free to pursue an independent course in international affairs to the bitter end. Non-nuclear powers win contests of will only on the sufferance of the USSR and the United States. In a true national life-or-death issue they would have to give way, unless they could secure U.S. and Soviet forebearance.

Fortunately, international conflicts are seldom pursued to the point of national survival or destruction. Such military action as has taken place since World War II has involved only conventional weapons. The era has not by any measure been a peaceful one, but no conflict has yet involved the actual employment of nuclear arms. The closest call was probably the Cuba missile crisis of October 1962, when Soviet inferiority in strategic weapons—delivery systems and U.S. superiority in conventional forces in the Caribbean forced the USSR into a humiliating withdrawal of its missiles.

It is clear that in such circumstances conventional military strength is the key to confrontations short of war. It also assures nations which are under attack from more aggressive neighbors that they can put up some defense until the nuclear powers can contain the conflict and adjudicate or arbitrate it. Up to a certain point, a nation with effective conventional military forces can even defy the restraining influence of the nuclear powers and triumph over less well-armed states. North Vietnam's takeover of South Vietnam, Cambodia, and Laos, in the face of the efforts of the United States to prevent it, is an eloquent demonstration of this point. The crucial difference, of course, probably was in varying levels of national will, but South Vietnam's armies were finally beaten on the battlefield with conventional weapons while the United States stood by.

Crucial Elements of Military Power

Perceptions of military power are highly subjective, but it is clear that a weighting system for military capability has to take into account two crucial elements. First, it must give primary importance to nuclear deterrence, either total, as in the case of the USSR and the United States, or limited, as in the case of the United Kingdom, France, and China. The perceived power of a nation is enhanced immeasurably if a nation's nuclear-weapons strength is sufficient to face conventional challenges right down to the last step into nuclear war without fear that its actual war-fighting capabilities in a nuclear exchange would prove so greatly inferior that the nation could not afford the risk of continuing the struggle. Only the USSR and the United States can pass this test at present.

Since most future conflicts will probably be fought with conventional non-nuclear forces, a second crucial element is the maintenance of respectable armies, navies, and air forces for general-purpose combat. While they are probably of use only in less than national life-or-death confrontations, this is the way all conflicts begin.

Conventional capability is doubly important because its use, or the threat of its use, guards the lower rungs of the ladder of escalation to nuclear warfare. A nation that can defend itself on even terms against a conventional thrust does not have to contemplate taking the awesome next step to nuclear war. In this chapter we will analyze only strategic nuclear forces, reserving the equally important assessment of conventional military forces to the next chapter.

The Political Pressures Exerted by Nuclear Weapons

When national leaders are compelled to consider the strength of the strategic forces at their disposal, in a crisis severe enough to present the risk of nuclear conflict, the question uppermost in their minds must be the damage that their societies could suffer in the event of war. Moreover, even when the possibility of actual conflict remains remote, as it will unless a nation's most vital interests are at stake, perceptions of each other's ultimate capabilities will limit the demands that national leaders feel free to make. It is impossible to forecast with confidence the interplay of move and countermove, but awareness of the risk of war, and a sense, however vague, of the ultimate balance of military strengths will act on men's minds and set tacit limits on their actions.

The limits on adversary actions set by direct nuclear deterrence are obvious enough. For example, it is quite clear that the leaders of the Soviet Union could not at present order an all-out attack on North American cities without facing the unacceptable prospect that Soviet cities would in turn be destroyed. If this, indeed, were the only practical implication of the strategic balance, we scarcely need bother to calculate the relative military capabilities of the United States and the Soviet Union, or, in fact, of any of the nuclear powers. No rational adversary would be likely to run the risk of provoking a nuclear attack on itself.

Deterrence depends upon the total balance of forces, not on the atmospherics of diplomatic exchanges. The current detente is often justified as preventing nuclear holocaust, but it is in fact a political relationship made possible by the rough parity of deterrent nuclear power of the U.S. and the Soviet military forces. Holding a population hostage in the face of a nuclear threat may confer very great political leverage, but only if the imminence of destruction is credible. Such leverage is automatically negated when the population of the aggressor is equally vulnerable, as in the case of the USSR and the United States.

Military planning must nevertheless proceed on the basis of a possible surprise attack, however remote its likelihood. If strike-back forces are adequate in that setting, they will serve to deter all-out attacks in any conceivable circumstance. Policy, on the other hand, cannot be formulated exclusively in terms of all-out attacks and all-out responses.

It is the danger that economic and political conflicts will escalate to the point where threats of nuclear war are implicit, that U.S. and Soviet policymakers must think about and with which they must be prepared to deal. The political-psychological pressure exerted by the mere existence of nuclear weapons is the significant element in international power calculations.

Recently the nuclear balance between the USSR and the United States has changed from a marked U.S. superiority over the USSR in strategic weapons to some rough equivalent of parity. Looking ahead, the United States will undoubtedly continue to maintain a reliable deterrent against direct nuclear attack, for at least five to ten years, but the Soviet Union will add some additional new capabilities, including "counterforce" attack options aimed at destroying the fixed land-based missiles of the United States, the People's Republic of China, and France. Well before this point is reached, the growing nuclear forces of the Soviet Union could acquire a margin of perceived superiority in the eyes of political leaders all over the world. This image of superior strength would enhance Soviet influence and prestige at the expense of the United States. Inevitably, the effect would be to induce third parties to try to conciliate Soviet demands at the expense of U.S. interests. In the sense of giving the USSR a tacit veto over the policies of other states, particularly nearby ones, this situation is often described as "Finlandization"; the classical term is neutralization. Military capability, if it is visible and overwhelming, can force former adversaries into an impotent neutrality.

Political judgments are based on gross and unsophisticated perceptions. It is not the opinion of technical experts that matters but rather the sometimes "unscientific" views of political leaders at home and abroad. Much of what follows deals with the factual aspects of the measurement of strategic power, but it should never be forgotten that military strategy is politics, not a branch of engineering.

Trends in Nuclear Weapons Strength

The perceptions that shape political evaluations and strategic plans are not fixed; they are dynamic. A growing and innovative arsenal will be perceived as more powerful than one which is static—even if the latter still retains an advantage in purely technical terms. This is perfectly appropriate because political practitioners must always attempt to anticipate future power trends and not base their policies on a static view of the present. The lead-time for development and production of modern advanced weapons is from five to ten years. Hence it is prudent to note the trend line and rate of change along with absolute numbers as of the present.[2]

A time graph showing numbers of the most visible and highly advertised strategic weapon, the intercontinental land-based missile, reveals a rather startling reversal of comparative U.S. and Soviet numerical strengths over a 15-year period.

Land-Based ICBMs: Actual Strengths

Year	USSR	U.S.
1960	35	18
1961	50	63
1962	75	294
1963	100	424
1964	200	635
1965	270	854
1966	300	904
1967	460	1,054
1968	800	1,054
1969	1,050	1,054
1970	1,300	1,054
1971	1,510	1,054
1972	1,550	1,054
1973	1,575	1,054
1974	1,590	1,054
1975	1,600	1,054
1976	1,550	1,054
1977	1,450	1,054

It is impossible to state precisely how the political leaders of the lesser powers measure strategic strength; certainly not by means of detailed numerical studies. More likely men's views of the military balance are impressionistic, based on images mainly qualitative in nature. Thus bombers may be thought of as "old-fashioned" regardless of how effective they may be in the calculations of professional analysts, while weapons publicly and repeatedly described as "giant ICBMs" and "supermissiles" make a deep impression which far transcends their actual military usefulness.

The clear-cut difference in the number of missiles allowed to each side in the 1972 SALT I Interim Agreement and Protocol had a considerable psychological impact, while the countervailing factors such as accuracy of guidance systems, whose importance is so obvious to the professional experts, went almost unnoticed. After the signature of the accords, even casual readers of the daily press learned, from constant repetition, that the United States was allowed to deploy only 1,054 ICBMs as against 1,618 for the Soviet Union and that the maximum limits on SLBMs were 710 for the United States and 950 for the Soviet Union. It was a far smaller number of observers who were aware of the substantial U.S. advantage in the number and combat quality of bombers, or in the number of separately deliverable nuclear warheads. Estimated strengths of major strategic weapons for mid-1977 are as follows:

Military Balance Sheet

U.S.		USSR
1,054	Intercontinental Missiles	1,450
656	Submarine-Launched Missiles	919
418	Strategic Bombers	210

Many nonexpert observers concluded that the United States had conceded a certain position of strategic superiority to the Soviet Union, and that the SALT I accords were therefore a clear signal of a decline in U.S. strategic power across the board. While Soviet superiorities in SALT I were seen as finite and contractual, the technological and qualitative advantages of the United States were usually perceived as a wasting asset, to be discounted in estimates of future power relationships.

In view of all these factors, to measure roughly the broad, quasi-psychological effects of power we are studying, we have adopted a weighting system for military capability that allows a maximum of ten perceived power weights, roughly equivalent to economic capability. A maximum of ten weights is allotted for effective nuclear deterrence based on nuclear war-fighting capability, and another maximum of ten for conventional military strength. Most of the nations of the world will qualify only in the latter category. Obviously, these weighted elements of perceived power can be calculated only in gross, macrometric terms. We present specific statistics only to anchor in detailed reality our own assessment of military capability as an instrument of national policy.

Measuring Nuclear Capabilities

The standard way of measuring the destructive effect of nuclear weapons is to calculate the equivalent force in conventional explosive material (TNT). This gives each weapon a yield of kilotons (thousands of tons of TNT) or megatons (millions of tons of TNT). In World War II the total of conventional bombs dropped by the U.S. Air Force amounted to only two megatons, the yield of one or two ordinary nuclear bombs today.

In trying to think about the unthinkable, military planners have devised more sophisticated methods of measuring actual weapons capabilities. One is to rate every weapon on the "one-megaton equivalent" scale, which measures the destructive power nuclear weapons would have if actually delivered on target. Like ordinary chemical explosions, nuclear detonations produce destructive effects which spread outward in all directions, with diminishing impact as distance increases. Targets are unavoidably over-destroyed at the core of the explosion, so that much of the energy yield of explosive weapons is wasted. The more powerful the device—other things being equal— the smaller the proportion of the energy yield which is actually effective on target. A simple formula can be used to convert the gross nominal yield of nuclear weapons in megatons or kilotons into one-megaton equivalents (o.m.e.), as a rough measure of real destructive power against surface targets, such as cities.

In a "city-busting" scenario, which lies at the heart of most early theory of strategic deterrence and certainly figures centrally in the popular imagination of nuclear war, the actual number of bombs or warheads that can be aimed at targets is very important. The United States has more aircraft and smaller missiles with multiple warheads. Hence it far outclasses the USSR at present in numbers of strategic weapons and megaton equivalence. The o.m.e. method is a measuring technique better suited to war-gaming and close-precision analysis of nuclear exchanges than to macrometric perceptions of military power. Numbers of weapons or what the U.S. Defense Department calls "force-loadings" make more sense to most observers.

U.S.-USSR Strategic Nuclear Weapons
(Bombs and Warheads)
("force-loadings")

There is another useful measurement, the calculation of throw-weight—or missile payload. Throw-weight figures tell us something useful, i.e., what a missile can carry to target. The delivery capacity of missiles, like the payload of bombers (at stated ranges), defines the ultimate potential capabilities of strategic forces.

Even without major new discoveries, the energy yield extracted from every pound of payload has been steadily augmented over the years as the technology of nuclear weapons has become increasingly refined. Similarly, accuracies have been improving as more refined guidance equipment is produced. Given these technological changes, in the long run the measure of strategic capability will be set by the capacity of the vehicles available to deliver payloads. This factor becomes especially important if numbers of missiles are limited by agreement (as in SALT I and II) but numbers of warheads are not.

As the USSR introduces increasing numbers of its three new multiple-warhead ballistic missiles into operational use, it will be working toward the ceilings prescribed in SALT II. At those high ceilings the USSR would increase its total throw-weight to about 12 million pounds, in land-based ICBM forces alone; the throw-weight of the U.S. ICBM force is now about 2 million pounds.[3] These ceilings will not be reached for several years, however, so the throw-weight advantage is a future or potential capability that does not alter the present balance.

Overall missile throw-weights would only measure actual capabilities, even in the future, if the missile and nuclear technologies of all sides were equally advanced, and if the strategic arsenals were oriented to the same goals. At the moment the United States appears to enjoy a significant, though diminishing, advantage in numbers of warheads, warhead yield/weight ratios, missile accuracies, booster efficiency, and electronic countermeasures (ECM) for bombers. In throw-weight, the United States is markedly inferior to the USSR, whose missiles and silos are much larger.

Since the early 1960s, the United States has deployed forces optimized for attacks on cities and other dispersed targets, as indicated by the very small warheads of the *Poseidon* submarine-launched missiles (40 kiloton) and the modestly sized (170 kiloton) warheads of newer ICBMs, the *Minuteman-3*s; a new (MK 12A) warhead of approximately 400 kilotons is being produced for the *Minuteman*. As against this, the Soviet Union has deployed some very large warheads (20-25 megaton nominal yield) on most of its "heavy" land-based missiles.

Numbers of Strategic Weapons

A simple numerical summary of the array of U.S. and Soviet weapons systems and strategic-nuclear forces is presented below. The characteristics of the new Soviet missile types just now beginning to be deployed are described on page 100. Probably about 140 SS-19s, 50 SS-18s, and 40 SS-17s, were deployed in the USSR as of January 1977. The United States, of course, has no new missiles to deploy.

The United States and the Soviet Union also have other means of long-range delivery that are often regarded as nonstrategic because they are qualitatively inferior or their performance is in some way limited. These include Soviet medium bombers which can reach U.S. territory on one-way missions only; U.S. tactical strike aircraft deployed in Europe and capable of reaching the USSR, and Soviet long-range cruise missiles on board nuclear and non-nuclear submarines. The United States has 7,000 nuclear weapons deployed in Europe and many more deployed at sea and at other military bases overseas in addition to some 9,000 nuclear weapons designated as strategic—a total of about 22,000. For its part, the Soviet Union deploys a large (about 600) force of "intermediate" (IRBM) and "medium" (MRBM) range ballistic missiles targeted on West Europe and China; these antiquated weapons are now being replaced by the variable-range SS-20.

Among the lesser nuclear powers, only France deploys a full "triad" of offensive forces; that is, intercontinental land-based missiles (ICBM), submarine-launched ballistic missiles (SLBM), and long-range bomber forces. The United Kingdom still retains a force of medium-range *"V"* bombers which could deliver nuclear weapons on the Soviet Union, but its only official strategic force consists of four ballistic-missile submarines. The People's Republic of China has not yet deployed a submarine element in its strategic arsenal but has a modest force of medium bombers and is slowly building a land-based missile force targeted on the Soviet Union. In addition, Chinese fighter-bombers capable of delivering nuclear weapons could reach Soviet and Indian targets. For the time being, India has only the capability of producing a handful of plutonium bombs which could no doubt be delivered on Chinese and Pakistani targets by aircraft. There is as yet no evidence of any Indian missile-development effort.

Defense Forces

There is an obvious imbalance between these vast offensive forces and the rather weak strategic defenses deployed on all sides, an imbalance that is historically unprecedented. In particular, there are no substantial missile defenses, probably because the USSR and the United States both calculated the costs were too massive and such defenses would only spur both sides to deploy ever more numbers of expensive and unneeded offensive missiles. Under the terms of the 1972 Anti-Ballistic Missile

Strategic-Nuclear Offensive Weapons Arsenals in Mid-1977

ICBMs—Intercontinental Ballistic Missiles	U.S.	USSR
Total ICBMs	1,054	1,450
"heavy"*	0	285
"old"	54	75
"light"	1,000	1,090
Fitted with multiple warheads (MRV)	0	61
Fitted with multiple, independently targetable warheads (MIRV)	550	210

SLBMs—Submarine-Launched Ballistic Missiles		
Total SLBMs (incl. under conversion)	656	919
SLBMs on "modern nuclear submarines"*	656	850
SLBMs on "older nuclear submarines"*	0	21
SLBMs on diesel-electric submarines	0	48
Fitted with MRV	176	some
Fitted with MIRV, operational	352	0
SLBMs counted as "strategic" under SALT I and Vladivostok tentative agreement rules	656	880

Manned Long-Range Bombers		
Total, gross inventories	602	360
Operational	418	210
Bombers counted as "strategic" under SALT I and Vladivostok tentative agreement rules	418	210
Total offensive delivery vehicles defined as "strategic" under Vladivostok tentative agreement rules	2,128	2,540

*SALT I definitions

(ABM) Treaty, as amended in 1974, the Soviet Union and the United States may each deploy only a single missile-defense complex, with no more than 100 interceptor missiles.

As against this abnegation of missile defenses, large air-defense forces consisting of ground-based radar networks, manned fighters, anti-aircraft (AA) missiles, and anti aircraft guns remain in service in the Soviet Union and China, while smaller air-defense forces, consisting primarily of manned interceptors, are deployed in the United States, the United Kingdom, and France, as in many other countries. These defensive forces have little effect on the strategic nuclear equation, particularly as far as the USSR and the United States are concerned.

A final element in strategic defenses, though one not usually designated as such, are the extensive antisubmarine-warfare (ASW) forces deployed by the major powers. There is no technical distinction between tactical (i.e., shipping protection) and strategic ASW, although operationally the use of the forces would be quite different. The United Kingdom, the Soviet Union, and the United States all deploy nuclear-powered attack submarines, the most effective single ASW weapon, though by its very nature any ASW campaign would have to be a coordinated effort involving land-based search aircraft, surface warships, and seabed acoustic sensor grids, as well as attack submarines. For the time being, the peculiar properties of seawater continue to limit the range and reliability of the most important detection equipment, sonar, in all its various forms. Ballistic-missile launching submarines, while by no means immune to attack, are relatively secure.

Land-Based Missiles

There has been a striking divergence between the land-based missile policies of the superpowers. Long before the signature of the SALT I accords, the United States made the momentous decision to abandon the development of intermediate-range missiles (IRBMs), to scrap existing forward-based ballistic missiles, and unilaterally to limit its deployment of intercontinental ballistic missiles (ICBMs) to 1,054 units.

Since that time, the United States has concentrated on qualitative improvements with the deployment of separately targetable multiple-warhead (MIRV) systems, improved accuracies, and, presumably, reliabilities, in a single type of ICBM, the *Minuteman-3*, first deployed in 1970.

As a result of this policy, and the rapidity with which older weapons were withdrawn, the United States retains in service fewer than half of the land-based ballistic missiles it has built over the years, even though

The Five Strategic
Nuclear Powers: 1977

Inventories of Manned Bombers
Submarine-launched Ballistic Missiles
and Land-based Ballistic Missiles

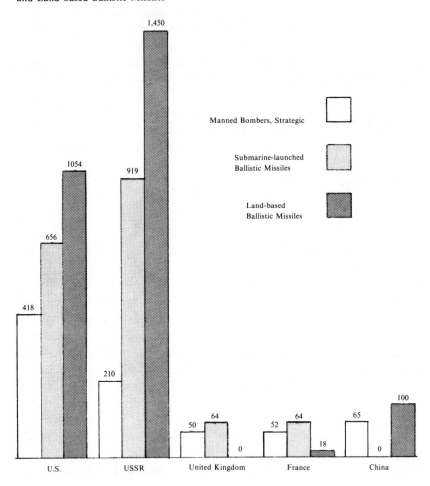

Manned Bombers, Strategic

Submarine-launched
Ballistic Missiles

Land-based
Ballistic Missiles

many of those scrapped were at least comparable to weapons which remain in the Soviet arsenal. In contrast, the Soviet Union has retained in service all but a few of the strategic missiles it has ever deployed; the purely numerical superiority of the Soviet ICBM force, which apparently counted for so much in the SALT negotiations, was largely a result of this policy. Shrewdly, the Soviet Union accorded a much higher priority to political visibility than to purely technical considerations.

If a weapon can reach deep into enemy territory to strike at homeland population centers, it is in a sense "strategic." If such a weapon is armed with a nuclear device, it becomes "strategic-nuclear," whether or not it has full intercontinental range. The Soviet medium- and intermediate-range ballistic missiles targeted on Europe and China fall within this class, even if they cannot reach U.S. targets, for without their deployment the Soviet Union would have to allocate ICBMs for this purpose.

There is a second feature of the Soviet ICBM deployment policy that is also in clear contrast to U.S. policy. Instead of concentrating the full range of Soviet technical advance in a single weapon type, at least three distinct classes of ICBMs have been produced: a small solid-fuel class, a medium-sized liquid-fuel class, and a heavy class. Even the medium-sized class has larger throw-weights than the U.S. *Minuteman-3,* and this, together with the numerical superiority of the Soviet ICBM force, has resulted in an altogether greater throw-weight capacity of the order of at least 6 million pounds for the Soviet Union versus 2 million for the United States, as mentioned previously. When the present Soviet launchers are replaced with planned newer models, the throw-weight of the Soviet force will be at least 10 and probably 12 million pounds, approximately a 5:1 or 6:1 advantage over the existing U.S. land-based ICBM force. That ratio will only be attained in the 1980s. There is still time for the United States, if it so chooses, to alter the trend.

The Soviet warhead development efforts which seek to translate the potential throw-weight advantage into actual strike capabilities have lagged behind, although the gap is being narrowed. Soviet MIRV systems reached the advanced testing stage only in 1974, and their first operational deployments took place only in mid-1975. (Details on U.S. and Soviet land-based ICBMs are shown in the chart on page 99.)

Mobile ICBMs are not strategically significant at present but they are potentially less vulnerable to counterforce attacks than are present fixed-site ICBMs housed in protected silos. This class of weapons, which is growing in importance, was not covered by the SALT I Interim

Agreement, nor was any prohibition on weapons of this class included in the tentative SALT II agreement, although it seems certain that restrictions will have to be imposed on their mode of deployment, in order to permit verification, if their numbers increase.

Many configurations for mobile ICBMs have been suggested: air-launched missiles deployed on aircraft held on ground alert, land-mobile deployments on road or rail networks, and closed-circuit land-mobile deployments, where ICBMs would rotate from shelter to shelter on rail or truck-like platforms inside secure areas. In the United States there are still some very large military reservations which could be used for the purpose, and, of course, both the Soviet Union and China would have no difficulty in finding vast and secure deployment areas.

There are both added costs and technical complications in mobile ICBM design. Nevertheless, should improvement in ICBM accuracies render fixed-site, land-based missiles very vulnerable to counterforce attacks, air- or land-mobile ICBMs may well be adopted in order to avoid exclusive dependence on submarine and manned bomber systems. Verification of arms limitations, however, would become exceptionally difficult in that circumstance. Cruise missiles are now in the same category, although the air-breathing subsonic cruise missiles now in advance development are much cheaper while being somewhat vulnerable to interception.

Aside from the considerable technical uncertainties inherent in our estimates of comparative U.S. and Soviet ICBM forces, U.S. policy confronts a deeper and politically more significant ambiguity as to the whole direction of the Soviet ICBM program. While the United States publishes its program years in advance, the Soviet Union makes nothing public, except for some general claims of superiority. Furthermore, even after several years of supposedly intimate negotiations, very little, if anything, has been learned about the goals and modalities of Soviet strategic policy. Thus, for example, it is not known what role the counterforce mission plays in Soviet policy—beyond what may be inferred from the evidence of past missile deployments, which suggests that this role is important. In fact, we have almost no information at all on Soviet strategic policy, only on actual capabilities.

U.S. and USSR ICBMs: Salient Features and Numbers Deployed, 1977

U.S.	Year First Deployed	Number Operational	Warhead Systems Number of	Yield Mt./Kt.	Throw Weight (1,000 lbs.)
Minuteman-2	1965	450	1	1 Mt.	2.5
Minuteman-3	1970	550	3 MIRV	170 Kt.	2.5
Titan-2	1963	54	1	9 Mt.	8.0
USSR					
"old"					
SS-7	1962	56	1	5 Mt.	7.0
SS-8	1963	19	1	5 Mt.	7.0
"light"					
SS-13	1969	60	1	1 Mt.	1
SS-16	1975		1 MIRV	1 Mt.+	2.0
"medium"					
SS-11 Mod. 1	1966	789*	1	1-2 Mt.	2.0
SS-11 Mod. 2/3	1973	61	3 MIRV	300 Kt.	2.0
SS-17	1975	40	4 MIRV	1 Mt.	2.0
SS-19	1975	140	6 MIRV	400 Kt.	6
"heavy"					
SS-9 Mod. 1/2	1967	235	1	20 Mt.	10-15
SS-18 Mod. 1	1974	20	1	20 Mt.	15
SS-18 Mod. 2	1976	30	8 MIRV	1 Mt.	15
MRBMs SS-4	1959	500	1	1 Mt.	
IRBMs SS-5	1961	100	1	1 Mt.	
SS-20	1976	(Full replacement of SS-4/SS-5s expected)			

*Figure is a residual; out of 1,450 deployed ICBMs, 285 "heavies" and 301 identified "lights" are subtracted; of the balance of 874 units, 75 are assumed "old" and the balance is assumed to be made up of SS-11 Mod. 1s.

There is no such uncertainty with respect to the Soviet SS-18, the most powerful ICBM ever built. This very large launcher has a throw-weight at least seven times that of the *Minuteman-3*. It represents a major military investment. Unless its development reflects bureaucratic irrationality of monumental proportions, it must have a purpose other than that of the common run of Soviet ICBMs. This purpose can only be to deliver a heavy-weight MIRV payload of several large individual warheads. It has been tested with seven MIRVs. The military role of such warheads is apparently to attack U.S. ICBM silos and command centers. The Soviet development of this counterforce-oriented missile must be viewed with concern in the West since it is inconsistent with the prevailing notion of strategic stability, which requires that something like present levels of retaliation—strikeback or second-strike capability—be predictable and assured for both sides so that deterrence for the prevention of war will be mutually reliable.

Owing to the more advanced state of U.S. warhead technology, which results in a more efficient use of launcher throw-weight, it is sometimes suggested that the latest U.S. land-based missile, *Minuteman-3*, is potentially a counterforce weapon and thus comparable to the giant Soviet SS-18. It is true that with very high accuracies a small warhead such as that of the *Minuteman-3* could be effective against Soviet ICBM silos. Indeed with the accuracies now commonly achieved by short-range precision-guided missiles, it would be possible to destroy heavily protected ICBM silos with warheads much smaller than those of the *Minuteman-3*. But it is one thing to guide an antitank rocket precisely to a target a few thousand yards away and quite another to launch ballistic warheads over ranges of thousands of miles. It is not difficult to imagine ways of dramatically improving present accuracies, given time and abundant resources, but so far no real attempt has been made in the United States to achieve any such results. The variety of research and development efforts to improve strategic ballistic missile accuracies has had the more modest goal of achieving refinements in existing guidance systems rather than to produce entirely new ones. Radical improvement would require warheads that have maneuverability and a good terminal guidance system.

The provisions of the SALT I Interim Agreement limit U.S. and Soviet ICBM forces to 1,054 and 1,618 units respectively. In addition, there is a sub-limit of 313 units on "heavy" missiles for the Soviet Union; the United States is allowed none. At the time, the sub-limit on "heavy" missiles seemed highly important, and indeed agreement on this provision was a central goal of the U.S. negotiating team. If the sub-limit on "heavy" ICBMs was obtained in exchange for the Soviet concession of the very high overall ICBM ceiling, on the assumption that only the "heavy" missiles had a counterforce potential then the benefits have been rather illusory. The counterforce potential, of the "medium" missiles, particularly the new MIRV SS-19, is not greatly inferior. Thus it is not clear that a sub-limit on "heavy" ICBMs will be retained, in the proposed ten-year treaty whose outlines were agreed on at Vladivostok, at an overall ceiling of 2,400 long-range bombers and missiles with a sub-limit of 1,320 on SLBMs and ICBMs fitted with MIRV systems.

Among the lesser nuclear powers, only China is proceeding with a full-scale land-based ballistic missile program. British efforts in this sector ceased more than a decade ago, and the French land-based missile force is limited to a planned total of 18 IRBMs. Although housed in protected silos, the French IRBMs are inevitably rather vulnerable. Since inaccuracy increases with range, Soviet weapons would have much higher kill probabilities against French IRBMs than against U.S. ICBM silos located further away. The French missile force, unlike the Soviet or the U.S. force, cannot offer assurance of retaliation.

The Chinese land-based missile program has advanced at a rather slower pace than was expected, especially with respect to full-range ICBM weapons. China remains a largely agrarian country, with only small islands of technical sophistication and modern industry. Moreover, there are indications that the Chinese are following a long-term development strategy rather than searching for quick-fix solutions. Large-scale facilities for producing nuclear materials are being built and substantial resources have been allocated to solid-fuel missile propulsion. In the meantime, China deploys perhaps 30 liquid-fuel MRBMs, which could reach cities in eastern Siberia, and a roughly similar number of storable-fuel IRBMs. Both weapons are of poor overall quality and have slow reaction times. Longer-range weapons, limited ICBMs which may become operational quite soon, though as yet they are virtually untested, and a full-sized ICBM which probably will not be ready until the 1980s, are under development. If present national policies are followed on all sides, the Chinese will most probably choose to concentrate their short-term efforts on the deployment of a fully reliable deterrent against Soviet nuclear coercion, or even attack, since a strategic force targeted on the United States could serve only second-order political goals for many years to come.

The present Chinese land-based missile force thus consists of first-generation weapons mostly poorly protected against a disarming counterforce strike. Unlike the French IRBM force, however, the Chinese ballistic missile force is a growing concern. By the time a Chinese ICBM force is fully developed, it is possible that all fixed-site weapons will have become vulnerable. The Chinese may therefore proceed directly, in the mid-1980s, to deploy solid-fuel mobile ICBMs (and SLBMs).

Submarine-Launched Ballistic Missiles

The shift in the balance of strategic forces between the Soviet Union and the United States has been most marked with regard to the submarine element. Until 1969, the absolute qualitative superiority of the U.S. ballistic missile submarine force was so great that its numerical superiority, although crushing, scarcely seemed to matter. From the beginning, the U.S. boats were equipped with solid-fuel *Polaris* missiles of great reliability, capable of underwater launch, and thus were able to target Moscow from vast areas of the North Atlantic as well as from the northern end of the Indian Ocean.

In contrast, the Soviet SLBM force was originally based on makeshift conversions of torpedo-firing attack submarines, vastly inferior to the *Polaris* type. With limited missile and launching capacities, Soviet submarines were also much less quiet in underwater cruise than U.S. boats. The diesel boats of course could not reach firing positions against U.S. territory without using their snorkel tubes, and were thus vulnerable to sonar and radar detection, and, therefore, attack. For these reasons the numerical advantage of the U.S. SLBM force, 656 versus approximately 130, understated the vast superiority of the forces. Even nonexpert political observers could perceive the qualitative advantages of the U.S. submarine force.

Since 1969, the United States has been converting existing *Polaris* boats to accommodate a new type of missile, the *Poseidon,* which can be up to ten times as effective as the *Polaris-A2* against cities, industrial centers, airfields, and other large unprotected targets, since it can carry ten MIRVs. The United States has maintained a self-imposed 41-boat limit on its submarine force, which was first attained in the course of 1967. The only recent change in the U.S. force will be the completion of the *Poseidon* conversion program; the last of the 41 *Poseidon*-equipped boats is due to enter service in 1977. This force provides, for the present and foreseeable immediate future, a guaranteed retaliatory—strike-back—capability which insures deterrence independently of land-based ICBM and bomber forces.

U.S. restraint in improving rather than expanding its SLBM force, together with a very rapid deployment program on the part of the Soviet Union, has enabled the Soviet Union to reverse the numerical superiority of the U.S. SLBM force while at the same time considerably reducing its qualitative advantage. Since 1968, 34 of the new Soviet *Y*-class nuclear-powered submarines have been deployed, and beginning in 1973 some of them were fitted with a new type of missile, the SS–N–8, which has a range substantially greater than the *Poseidon* and is probably intended for MIRVing.[4] In 1974, a modified boat, the *D-I,* came into use and by 1975, a new boat, the *D-II,* was observed under construction. The latter is fitted to carry 16 tubes for the new submarine-launched missile (SS–N–8).

The pace and diversity of Soviet SLBM deployment efforts have not been hampered by the SALT I accords. The latter set a final limit of 950 allowable SLBM tubes on board nuclear-powered submarines for the USSR, as against 710 units for the United States. Even some of those observers who welcomed the SALT I accords and who saw the land-based missile imbalance as reasonable in the light of U.S. superiority in the bomber sector, were disturbed by the provisions covering the SLBM forces. Aside from the gross and highly visible inequality in the final ceilings, the provisions for substitution were highly favorable to the USSR.

The SALT I Protocol set the level of the Soviet SLBM force on board nuclear submarines at 740 tubes, which seemed high to most informed U.S. observers, and allowed the 950-tube ceiling to be reached by scrapping 210 older Soviet ICBMs or older SLBMs. The United States, on the other hand, could only add 54 tubes by scrapping the existing and more effective *Titan-2* force.

Under the terms of the Vladivostok agreement-in-principle, a total of 2,400 SLBMs, ICBMs, and long-range bombers may be deployed by each side including up to 1,320 launchers fitted with MIRVs. It is unclear to what extent these limits will cause additional SLBMs to be deployed by each side. As far as the United States is concerned, the *Ohio*-class submarine program calls for the deployment of 11 boats, with a total of 264 tubes for *Trident* missiles. If these were added to the force, SLBMs would account for 920 of the 2,400 total and 760 of the 1,320 MIRVed launcher sub-limit. By 1980, the first *Polaris* boats will be approaching their twentieth year of continuous operation. If the increasing threat to land-based ICBMs prompts a shift from *Minutemen* to SLBMs (and/or cruise missiles), this could mean that more *Tridents* would be deployed. A third and attractive alternative would be the deployment of a smaller, slower, and cheaper submarine than the fast 18,700-ton *Trident*.

U.S. and USSR SLBM Forces:
Salient Features and Numbers in Inventory, 1977

Submarines

	Propulsion	Year First Deployed	Number in Inventory	SLBM Tubes
U.S.				
George Washington/ Ethan Allen (*Polaris*)	nuclear	1960	10	16
Lafayette Class (*Poseidon*)	nuclear	1963	31	16
USSR				
G-class*	diesel	1960	20	3
H-class	nuclear	1964	7	3
Y-class	nuclear	1968	34	16
D-I class	nuclear	1973	12	12
D-II class	nuclear	1974	10	16

SLBMs

	Year First Deployed	Range N. Miles	Number in Inventory (Incl. under Conversion)	Warhead Systems Number of	Yield Mt./Kt.
U.S.					
Polaris A-3	1964	2,500	176	3 MRV	200 Kt.
Poseidon C-3	1971	2,500	480	10 MIRV	40 Kt.

	Year First Deployed	Range N. Miles	Number in Inventory (Incl. under Conversion)	Warhead Systems	
				Number of	Yield Mt./Kt.
USSR					
SS-N-4	1960	350	24	1	1-2 Mt.
SS-N-5	1963	700	45**	1	1-2 Mt.
SS-N-6 Mod. 1	1968	1,300		1	1-2 Mt.
SS-N-6 Mod. 2	1974	1,600	555***	1	1-2 Mt.
SS-N-6 Mod. 3	1974	1,600		3 MRV	500 Kt. (estimated)
SS-N-8	1973	4,200	304	1	2 Mt.+

*These boats are not defined as "strategic" under the SALT definitions.
**Of which 21 are housed in *H*-class boats and 24 in *G-II* class boats. (Only the former are counted in the official listing of strategic forces.)
***Including 11 SS-6s assumed on (4) *G*-class submarines.

The 950-unit SLBM force-level set by the SALT I agreement opened a wide range of deployment options to the USSR, though the limit of 62 on the number of modern submarines would evidently become an operative constraint, just as the SALT I limit of 44 constrains the United States. No more *Y*-class boats are likely to be built beyond the 34 now operational, though their missiles will no doubt be upgraded. It is almost certain that the USSR will exercise its exchange option under Article III of the Interim Agreement, replacing older ICBMs with modern SLBMs, but it is not yet clear what the mixture of *D-I*s and *D-II*s will be.

It seems probable that in 1977 or soon thereafter the last of the antiquated Soviet submarines, which are grossly uneconomical as missile platforms, will be withdrawn. The characteristics and numbers of SLBMs now in inventory in the Soviet and U.S. Navies are the best guide to future developments.

Both the United Kingdom and France have followed the superpowers in deploying SLBMs on board nuclear-powered submarines, albeit in much smaller numbers. But while the former received complete missile launchers and other technical aid from the United States, the French program was based very largely on purely domestic technology. Owing to this fact, the French effort has resulted in the slower deployment of less capable forces, at considerably higher cost, than the British program. The British force of four boats, with a total of 64 tubes, is now in service. The French submarines also have 16 tubes each and under current plans a total of five (and perhaps six) boats are to be deployed. At present four boats are in service.

The People's Republic of China has had a single G-class boat for many years but without missiles. Work on a nuclear-powered submarine continues, but its mission, date of completion, and operational worth are unknown. So far, Chinese strategic missiles have been based on liquid-fuel launchers, which are not suitable for deployment on board submarines. The Chinese are developing solid-fuel launcher technology, essential for effective SLBMs. It is possible of course that China may take a different approach to the problem of fixed-site missile vulnerability, and, instead of going to sea in submarines, develop land-mobile ballistic missiles as mentioned above. Given the size of the Chinese mainland, a mobile system for IRBMs or ICBMs would be quite feasible (which is not the case for the United Kingdom or France). It obviously would be much cheaper to rotate IRBMs or even ICBMs on moving platforms than to keep them at sea, inside exceedingly expensive nuclear-powered submarines.

Manned Long-Range Bombers

Manned bombers belong to the only category of strategic weapons in which the United States still retains a net superiority, both qualitative and quantitative. This is true in spite of the fact that no new heavy bomber type has been deployed in the United States since the first B-52s became operational in 1955. The more modern medium bombers introduced later, the B-58 and the FB-111A, have not proved entirely successful as strategic weapons carriers. Accordingly the B-52s have repeatedly been upgraded with improved electronics, structural reinforcement of airframes, and lately with some very effective air-to-ground weapons.

The key to bomber penetration against current air defenses is not mere speed but rather low-level flight to evade radar detection and electronic-warfare (EW) capabilities. It is for this reason that tankers are deployed alongside the bombers; even the B-52s need refueling for optimal low-altitude performance. In any case, the B-52 has proved superior to more recently built supersonic aircraft.

Now, however, in the B-1 program, the United States is developing an aircraft which is both a full-sized intercontinental bomber with a theoretical payload almost twice that of the *B-52* and one which is supersonic. Ordinarily the *B-1s*, like the *B-52s*, would penetrate air defenses in low-altitude subsonic flight in order to underfly ground-based radar. The first *B-1s* will become operational at the end of the decade, assuming that there are neither technical problems nor policy changes.

There are in addition the carrier-based fighter-bombers and attack aircraft of the U.S. Navy deployed with the Sixth and Seventh Fleets. Theoretically these could penetrate Soviet or Chinese airspace. They could bomb the cities of the Soviet Southwest and those adjacent to the Northwest Pacific with substantial payloads. U.S. aircraft carriers have nuclear weapons on board, and their primary tactical aircraft could serve as backup elements in strategic target attacks.

The Soviet Union's manned bomber forces have been assigned a much lower priority than the ICBM or SLBM forces in Soviet defense strategy. Two heavy bomber models, the *Tu-95* turboprop and the *Mya-4* jet were first deployed operationally in 1956 and both have been produced in small numbers since then.

In addition to these bombers, which have a full intercontinental range, the USSR also has large numbers of medium bombers (*Tu-16s*) which do not have a primary strategic role against the United States. Their primary targets are almost certainly in West Europe and China. The real deficiency of these bombers, shared by the heavy bombers, is neither the range/payload limitation nor their subsonic speed, but rather the inadequacy of their supporting ECM equipment and the lack of effective air-to-ground missiles.

Many observers assume that Soviet disinterest in the bomber sector of the strategic competition will continue and that this reflects a negative Soviet judgment on the effectiveness of the manned bomber in the missile age. However, the deployment of a new supersonic heavy bomber, the *Backfire,* which, like the projected U.S. *B-1,* has variable-sweep wings, suggests that the Soviet policy on bombers has been reappraised. The *Backfire* is smaller than the *B-1,* but its range is definitely sufficient to allow the conduct of strategic nuclear missions against the United States, given airborne refueling. The *Backfire* is now in production and some 100 aircraft are already operational. There is no evidence that the Soviet Union will deploy this aircraft as an intercontinental strategic weapon, but there is no way of being certain that it will not do so.

Under the tentative provisions of the Vladivostok agreement-in-principle, a bomber counts as a single weapon within the overall weapon ceiling of 2,400 units. The sub-limit on MIRVed launchers does not apply. It seems, however, that any missile carried on board aircraft with a range greater than 600 kilometers would count against the overall weapon ceiling, while bombers equipped with such longer-range missiles are counted as MIRVed weapons. This provision, if carried over into the actual ten-year treaty, would have a direct bearing on the U.S. cruise-missile program. Unlike ballistic missiles, cruise missiles fly within the atmosphere much as ordinary manned aircraft. Development programs are underway for long-range cruise missiles which would come under the 2,400 Vladivostok weapons ceiling and whose launcher aircraft would come under the 1,320 MIRVed vehicle ceiling.

Current U.S. plans call for the deployment of 495 of the 2,400 allowable weapon units to be taken up by bombers (251 *B-52*s and 244 *B-1*s), a reasonable figure since it would allow for the retention of the present 656-unit SLBM force, the addition of 240 *Trident* SLBM tubes, and the maintenance of the deployed force of 1,000 *Minuteman* missiles.

The tentative Vladivostok rules define the U.S. *FB-111A* and the Soviet *Backfire* bombers as "nonstrategic," as well as the old Soviet *Tu-16*. For comparative purposes, however, they are listed on the following table showing Soviet and U.S. manned bombers.

U.S. and USSR Manned Bomber Forces

	Year First Deployed	Number mid-1977 Operational	Unrefueled Max. Range (Statute Miles)	Theoretical Max. Payload (Pounds)
U.S.				
B-52 G&H	1959	241	12,500	75,000
B-52 D	1956	80	9,000	60,000
FB-111A	1969	66	3,800	37,500
B-1	1980(?)			150,000
USSR				
Tu-95	1956	105	8,000	40,000
Mya-4	1956	35	6,000	20,000
Tu-16	1955	475	4,000	20,000
Backfire	1975	100	5,000	20,000

British, French, and Chinese Bombers

During the 1950s, the United Kingdom undertook an ambitious bomber program based on the innovative *"V"* bombers. Now, however, all but 48 have been withdrawn from service or converted to other uses, and the remaining force has been reassigned to tactical missions. In theory, therefore, the British no longer have a strategic bomber force, but the United Kingdom retains a large stock of nuclear weapons, and all of its remaining fighter-bombers deployed in the Federal Republic of Germany could reach targets in the Soviet Union.

France's bomber force, the first element in the French mini-triad in point of time, deployed as of 1964, consists of 36 operational *Mirage-IV*s. These are small supersonic aircraft which require mid-air refueling to reach targets such as Moscow on two-way missions. U.S.-built tanker aircraft are available for this purpose. Owing to its small payload, the French bomber force lacks adequate ECM capabilities, while its fuel limitation prevents sustained low-level flight at high speed.

So far, the Chinese have not flight-tested a strategic bomber of local design, but have a force of 65 *Tu-16*s in service, which could reach Moscow on one-way missions from inland airfields in China. Chinese light bombers and locally produced fighter bombers all have some degree of penetration capability against Soviet targets east of the Urals. Although numerically small and technically obsolescent by superpower standards, the Chinese bomber force remains important, since the only other strategic delivery vehicles of the Chinese, the land-based missiles, remain vulnerable to attack.

In the case of India and other potential third-level nuclear powers, manned aircraft are likely to prove the cheapest and most easily available means of nuclear delivery. A wide variety of aircraft, including ordinary fighter bombers with reasonable payloads, can attempt the nuclear delivery mission against targets territorially adjacent and not protected by sophisticated air defenses. Although this mission is not particularly exacting, an improvised force of aircraft can offer only a moderate possibility of success. A reliable delivery capability requires special training and much supporting equipment is essential. At the present time China has neither of these prerequisites and India is even less well provided.

Conclusion: Perceived Nuclear Power Weights

It is clear that the United States and the USSR now have unique strategic nuclear forces. They possess at present a near-absolute deterrent capability and a roughly equivalent capability for waging a nuclear war in the event that one—most irrationally—occurs. By comparison, China, the United Kingdom, and France have only minimal capabilities, sufficient perhaps to deter direct attacks by the major nuclear powers where the interests in dispute are marginal for the latter. In recent years the USSR has closed a wide strategic gap and has reached parity with the United States. At present the nuclear power of the two military giants is roughly equivalent. The crude weighting for our assessment is as follows:

Perceived Strategic Weapons Strength, 1977

Country	Nuclear Deterrence and War Fighting
USSR	100
United States	100
United Kingdom	10
France	10
China (PRC)	10

CHAPTER FIVE

Military Capability: The Conventional Force Balance
$P_p = (C + E + M) \times (S + W)$

T he destructive power of nuclear arms is immense, but for this very reason their use is also highly circumscribed. Only in the most desperate circumstances could nuclear weapons be rationally employed as military instruments, and it is therefore only in the most intense crises that strategic-nuclear forces can credibly serve as the tacit weapons of diplomacy.

Since 1945 none of the nuclear powers has found itself in a predicament that justified the employment of man's most awesome weapons. By now they are so numerous in U.S. and Soviet arsenals that the thought of a full exchange staggers the imagination. While there is no denying the tremendous psychological and political pressure exerted by nuclear powers, perceptions of military capability are equally affected by the implicit threat constituted by conventional armed forces.[1] Conventional, i.e., non-nuclear, forces have been used in combat with some frequency in the past three decades. Both in Korea and Vietnam the United States felt constrained to use only its non-nuclear military power. In the Mideast several wars, large and small, have been fought between Arab and Israeli and between Arab and Arab. In South Asia, two Indo-Pakistani wars have changed the map of the subcontinent and brought forth the new state of Bangladesh. In Africa, most recently, military intervention by Cubans with Soviet arms has determined the political fate of Angola.

In all these instances war has been conducted in the classic manner, as the final sanction of political conflict, whether domestic or international or both. Since conventional non-nuclear forces can still be used in actual warfare, the perceived power of nations possessing such forces remains a valid diplomatic instrument of policy on the international scene. Inherently flexible and thus usable in doses large or small in all manner of ways, non-nuclear capabilities can therefore be directly translated into international power.

Standard estimates of conventional military power, based mainly on manpower figures, combat units, and equipment inventories, are notoriously unreliable. In formulating these estimates, units and weapons are laboriously counted and great efforts are made to obtain the raw data on which the statistics are based; by contrast, the "intangibles" of military power, such as troop skill and morale, the quality of military leadership, the coherence of operational strategies, and the supreme intangible of political morale, cannot be counted and listed, and thus tend to be ignored. These intangibles are of course very difficult to define, and cannot be evaluated by any fixed and objective criteria, but estimates of military power which exclude them for this reason are not merely inadequate but misleading. In the actual reality of war, the intangibles count for as much or more than the number of men or the quantity of equipment—and in the case of equipment its quality often counts for more than mere quantity. In the Vietnam conflict, as in all the Arab-Israeli wars, statistical estimates have been grossly misleading as indicators of actual employable military powers.

A compilation of worldwide military statistics is largely irrelevant to this survey of military power on the international scene. Most of the world's 158 independent states keep armed forces primarily to control their own populations. Never deployed in war, rarely exercised for combat in the field, and mainly equipped with light weapons, these armed units are in reality police forces. Some genuine military capability is of course still inherent in these forces, but in most cases such capabilities are limited to purely defensive operations, in protection of national territory. Hence most of the world's armed forces are not instruments of international power, except insofar as they may negate the offensive forces of others.

To evaluate actual combat capabilities, subjective judgments must inevitably be made if the intangibles are to be taken into account. In this book we are attempting this difficult task by applying a series of "conversion factors" to basic troop strengths in a way designed to translate the statistics of manpower and weapons into units of estimated military power which can be compared internationally. Beginning with the universal base of the gross manpower figures of all military services (full-time only), perceived combat capabilities are calculated on the basis of an average conversion factor, made up of four distinct elements:

1. **Manpower Quality:** This factor is not meant to represent the human worth of the men and women in the armed forces concerned but merely their operational effectiveness in war. This is primarily a function of troop training and unit morale (not national morale, which depends on the particular circumstances of each separate conflict), as well as of officer leadership. The latter, often of crucial importance, will reflect the sociology of the officer corps more than anything else. It is therefore a very inflexible constraint on military strength: weapons can be bought overnight and troops can be trained in a year or two, but it takes a lifetime in the right environment to school officers with reliable skills and motivation.

2. **Weapon Effectiveness:** This factor takes due account of the quantity and quality of the weapons deployed, but only in the context of the armed forces concerned. It therefore differs from weapon efficiency, which is a function of the mechanical capability of tanks, guns, ships, and aircraft. In the case of quite a few armed forces, actual combat capabilities can decline when more sophisticated weapons are brought into service. For example, the wealthy but primitive oil-producing states of the Middle East are now in some cases equipping their forces with weapons which they cannot use at all; had they bought simpler weapons they would have had some real military capability because simpler weapons could be handled correctly by their manpower—unlike the advanced fighters, complex tanks, and large warships now being purchased. By contrast, some armed forces with advanced military skills are notoriously underequipped, the most notable case being the Canadian air forces.

3. **Infrastructure and Logistic Support:** This third factor covers a very wide field, from the adequacy of radar surveillance and control systems to the provision of aircraft shelters, and from the operation of repair units in the field to the adequacy of supply stocks. Most of the armed forces of the world rely on imported weapons and supplies. Routine estimates of military power do not differentiate between weapons locally produced and those which are imported; nor do they separate local supplies of the "consumables" (e.g., ammunition), from

those which are imported. But unless stocks are inordinately high, dependence on others amounts to a major detraction from national military power. Hence the state which is more self-sufficient in the necessities of war must be counted as the more powerful, other things being equal. Nonindustrial infrastructures, from naval port installations to ground control systems for the command of combat aircraft, together with military communication systems, now absorb a great deal of military expenditure; allowance for these must also be made under this heading.

4. **Organizational Quality:** The fourth and last conversion factor is intended to reflect the qualities of armed forces as bureaucratic organizations that must be supervised (managerial efficiency), must maintain at all times a certain level of capability available on call (readiness), and must make detailed step-by-step plans to implement their recognized missions (tactical planning). A key ingredient in all of these is relevant combat experience; war introduces realism in the life of large military organizations. In peacetime, armed forces often tend to drift away from reality as they cultivate their own bureaucratic urges and perpetuate their own past traditions, including those that are no longer functional. War imposes the discipline of reality on these organizational drives, correcting the drift to the extent that the crises of the conflict are severe.

Perceived Combat Capabilities

The application of these conversion factors yields the estimated units of perceived combat capability[2] set forth in the tables that follow. The tables begin with the Soviet Union and the Warsaw Pact states, and the United States with its NATO allies. Other nations with military forces totalling more than 100,000 are also evaluated in tables organized on a regional basis. In each case, some evaluations are explained in the text appended to each table, although it must be clear at the outset that the weighting is highly subjective and subject to argument.

Direct comparisons of the Warsaw Pact/USSR totals with the NATO/U.S. totals do not in themselves reflect the balance of armed strength in Europe. Aside from the commitments of Soviet and American forces elsewhere, alliance-wide capabilities cannot be computed by mere addition: further judgments must be introduced to take into account the degree of strategic and tactical coherence of the forces involved, the degree of equipment coordination and, above all, the difference in the degree of combat motivation. The Warsaw Pact is a centralized and Soviet-controlled system which would have the very great advantage of fully standardized equipment and full unity of command. NATO, by contrast, is a voluntary alliance and its armies have variegated equipment and tactics. Above all, NATO is subject to the contending pressures of different national governments. On the other hand, the Soviet Union cannot unfailingly count on the loyalty of Warsaw Pact troops; liable to be carried along by the *elan* of victory if things go well, Czech, Hungarian, Polish, and East German troops may turn on the Russians if difficulties are met. In the Rumanian case, major participation in offensive operations against NATO is unlikely.

The capsule picture of opposing combat forces along the lines of confrontation in Central Europe indicates that NATO has 734,000 troops, 6,430 tanks, 1,700 tactical aircraft, and 7,000 tactical nuclear warheads; in comparison the Warsaw Pact forces include approximately 900,000 troops, 15,700 tanks, 3,000 tactical aircraft and 3,500 tactical nuclear warheads. These numbers exclude Soviet forces deployed in the European region of the USSR and along the border of China.[3]

In the past ten years the USSR has deployed five divisions in Czechoslovakia, which had none before the crisis of 1968, and has modernized and strengthened all of its Central European forces substantially. Tactical aircraft have been greatly upgraded in performance. Tanks deployed with troops in this region have increased by about 40 percent, and the artillery by more than 50 percent.[4]

It is psychologically significant that NATO experts only argue about the length of time involved for Soviet conventional military forces to reach the Rhine if they launch an all-out attack (usually 48 hours to six days), and advance strategic warning of attack is no longer confidently expected to be received in time to make much difference. Thus most observers perceive an image of dynamic growth in Soviet military capability for military attack in Europe (with tactical nuclear units in reserve), something that cannot be quantified although it clearly aggrandizes perceptions of Soviet military capability. The situation is not grossly unequal for NATO, however, and the deterrent provided by tactical nuclear weapons still inhibits a Soviet attack. In a general evaluation of all military capabilities worldwide, the European balance

TABLE I
Non-Nuclear Military Forces :
Estimates of Equivalent Combat Capabilities

Warsaw Pact	Total Manpower (Thousands)	Manpower Quality	Weapon Effectiveness	Infrastructure & Logistics	Organizational Quality	Average	Equivalent Units of Combat Capability
USSR	4,400	0.7	0.9	0.7	0.5	0.7	3,080
Poland	300	0.6	0.7	0.6	0.5	0.6	180
East Germany (GDR)	204	0.9	0.8	0.6	0.7	0.8	163
Rumania	191	0.5	0.6	0.6	0.4	0.5	96
Czechoslovakia	190	0.8	0.8	0.6	0.4	0.7	133
Bulgaria	177	0.6	0.7	0.6	0.5	0.6	106
Hungary	120	0.8	0.7	0.6	0.5	0.7	84

Total, gross manpower: 5,582,000   Total, equivalent units of combat capability: 3,842 of power is not decisive and it is necessary to fall back on the method outlined above to build a table for the individual Warsaw Pact and NATO nations (see Table I).[5]

In the above, as in all subsequent conversion tables, the manpower total is meant to exclude civilians in uniform, here defined as personnel which in the U.S. forces would in fact be civil service (or contract) employees. By contrast, all forces which are equipped in a military manner and which serve full time are added to the official armed forces total. In the case of the non-Soviet Warsaw Pact manpower totals, internal security troops and all types of part-time militia forces are excluded, while border troops are included, if known to be equipped in a military manner. In the Soviet case KGB troops (not all KGB personnel) are included, as are MVD troops, since both are equipped with heavy weapons; in the Polish case only a fraction of the border troops are included, since most are equipped only for police duties. The "Manpower Quality" factor reflects primarily the proportion of peasant conscripts in the forces.

It will be noted that even the Soviet Union is not given a 100 percent weapon effectiveness rating, although its arsenal of all types is very large indeed. This is because it is the Soviet practice to keep obsolescent weapons in service (*MIG-17* fighters, *T-34* tanks, etc.) alongside newer models. It is also true that even quite new Soviet weapons are usually qualitatively inferior to their Western counterparts. In fact a straight quality comparison would have resulted in a much lower rating than 0.9, but quantity has been taken into due account, as has the suitability of simpler weapons to Soviet conditions. The weapon inventories of the Warsaw Pact armies are certainly very large, as Table II indicates.

Much more is known about Western armed forces than is the case for the Soviet and Warsaw Pact forces, but this does not make the problem of evaluation any easier, since NATO forces are so diverse. How is one to rate the well-known qualities of the Turkish soldier as an individual fighting man against the higher skill-levels of Danish troops? And what can be the comparison between the inventory of Italian weapons—some of good design but more not—as against that of Greek forces, which now have some very modern weapons alongside a residue of 1950s equipment? Here, as elsewhere, each conversion factor has to be justified in detail as a subjective judgment about specific components of combat capability (see Table III).

With the exception of the West German border police, which is in

TABLE II
Total Worldwide Warsaw Pact Weapon Inventories: Selected Indicator Items

Modern Tanks, Aircraft, and Warships in Operational Units

	Fighter Class Aircraft	Main Battle Tanks	Major Warships and Nuclear Submarines (attack)
USSR	6,600	35,000	103
Bulgaria	100	2,000	0
Czechoslovakia	250	3,500	0
East Germany (GDR)	360	2,400	0
Hungary	110	1,000	0
Poland	400	3,000	0
Rumania	150	1,500	0

Definitions:

Fighter-class aircraft in operational squadrons: MIG-21s, Su-9s, Su-11s, (Su-7 mod.), Yak-28Ps, Tu-28Ps, Su-15S, Su-19S, MIG-23s, are all included whether serving in tactical commands or air defense forces; *MIG-15s, MIG-17s* and *MIG-19s* excluded.

Main battle tanks: Operational, *T-54s, T-55s, T-62s,* and *T-72s* are included but *T-34s* are excluded.

Major warships: Modern missile-armed cruisers and larger air-capable ships are included, older gun cruisers and all vessels under 6,000 tons are excluded; all nuclear attack boats included, regardless of age.

effect a well-equipped light infantry force, and of some carabinieri units whose equipment compares favorably with that of the Italian army, NATO manpower totals include only regular armed force personnel. It will be noted that although the United States fought a long war in Vietnam, the organizational quality factor is rated at only 0.8, because much of the Vietnam experience is apt to be misleading if applied directly to other theaters. The conversion factors for weapon effectiveness would have been lower in the recent past than now for the most poorly armed NATO members, Greece and Turkey. Both have been re-equipping their forces, seemingly more willing to arm against each other than they were to arm against the Soviet Union. The conversion factor for manpower quality naturally stresses officer leadership quality; the values might have been different if they reflected only the quality of the rank-and-file (see Table IV).

TABLE III
Non-Nuclear Military Forces:
Estimates of Equivalent Combat Capabilities

United States and NATO	Total Manpower (thousands)	Manpower Quality	Weapon Effectiveness	Infrastructure & Logistics	Organizational Quality	Average	Equivalent Units of Combat Capability
United States	2,086	1	1	0.9	0.8	0.9	1,877
West Germany(FRG)	515	1	0.9	0.9	0.7	0.9	464
France	513	0.8	0.7	0.8	0.6	0.7	359
Turkey	490	0.7	0.5	0.4	0.5	0.5	245
Italy	362	0.6	0.5	0.5	0.4	0.5	181
United Kingdom	344	1	0.8	0.8	0.7	0.8	275
Greece	200	0.7	0.5	0.4	0.5	0.5	100
Netherlands	112	0.9	0.8	0.8	0.6	0.8	90
Belgium	88	0.9	0.8	0.8	0.6	0.8	70
Canada	78	0.9	0.6	0.6	0.6	0.7	55
Portugal	60	0.7	0.2	0.2	0.6	0.4	24
Norway	39	0.9	0.8	0.6	0.6	0.7	27
Denmark	35	0.8	0.6	0.6	0.4	0.6	21

Total, gross manpower: **4,922,000**   Total, equivalent units of combat capability: **3,788**

TABLE IV
Total Worldwide NATO and U.S. Weapon
Inventories: Selected Indicator Items

Modern Tanks, Aircraft, and Warships in Operational Units

	Fighter-Class Aircraft	Main Battle Tanks	Major Warships and Nuclear Submarines
United States	6,200	9,600	109
Belgium	145	330	0
United Kingdom	425	900	15
Canada	130	70	0
Denmark	110	200	0
France	400	1,050	4
West Germany (FRG)	450	4,000	0
Greece	180	725	0
Italy	170	660	3
Netherlands	170	800	0
Norway	125	115	0
Portugal	0	0	0
Turkey	300	1,000	0

Definitions:

Fighter-class aircraft in operational squadrons, Air Force, Navy, Marine, and air-defense aircraft, are all included if they are supersonic fighter-interceptors or Mach-2 air superiority fighters; modern attack aircraft are included (even if subsonic); thus the *F-84s, Etendard, Super-Mystere* and *G-91s* still in NATO service are excluded, while *F-4, F-5, F-104* and *Mirage* series aircraft are included as are *Lightnings, A-4s, A-7s, Jaguar,* and *Draken* aircraft.

Main Battle Tanks in operational units, *Leopard,* modernized *Centurion, Chieftan,* and *AMX-30* tanks, are all included as are *M-48* and *M-60* series tanks, but *M-47s* are not included.

Major Warships and Nuclear Submarines: all nuclear attack boats are included, as are missile-armed cruisers, aircraft carriers, and other large air-capable ships, including amphibious assault ships.

The neutral (or at least not formally allied) states of western and southern Europe include no major military powers although at least one, Sweden, has considerable military potential. Listed together with the European neutrals in Table V are the armed forces of Latin America. In both cases the smallest armed forces are excluded (i.e., forces with a total manpower below 100,000). In all cases, heavily-armed police "field units," and other militarized security forces have been added to the official total of armed force personnel.

TABLE V
Non-Nuclear Military Forces:
Estimates of Equivalent Combat Capabilities

European Neutrals and Latin America	Total Manpower (thousands)	Manpower Quality	Weapon Effectiveness	Infrastructure & Logistics	Organizational Quality	Average	Equivalent Units of Combat Capability
Spain	302	0.7	0.5	0.5	0.4	0.5	151
Yugoslavia	250	0.7	0.5	0.5	0.4	0.5	125
Switzerland*	247	0.9	0.5	0.6	0.5	0.6	148
Sweden*	200	1	1	1	0.6	0.9	180
Brazil	257	0.2	0.4	0.4	0.2	0.3	77
Cuba	175	0.2	0.5	0.2	0.3	0.3	53
Argentina	133	0.4	0.3	0.4	0.2	0.3	40

*In the case of Sweden and Switzerland those trained reserves which are annually recalled for refresher training are included.

In recent years, the military balance in the Mid-East has been a matter of international concern since local wars fought for local reasons have had worldwide repercussions. Conventional estimates of military power would show drastic changes in the region over time, with its vast inflow of military equipment—which has notably accelerated since the 1973 oil crisis. But in fact, in this equipment-rich area, it is the human and organizational factors which determine real-life military capabilities, and these are apt to change only over the span of decades as one generation replaces another. As the war of 1967 showed, the region contains in Israel at least one military power which would be of world caliber if its demographic base were not so small; as the war of 1973 was later to reveal, it also contains in Egypt a solid nation-state of sufficient military resilience to pass the test of a battlefield defeat without collapse.

Again the smaller armed forces, with less than 100,000 troops in all, have been excluded from the evaluation. Also shown in Table VI together with the armed forces of North Africa and the Mid-East are the two more substantial powers of sub-Saharan Africa. Nigeria, with its population, oil wealth, and considerable societal development, clearly has significant military potential, but its present armed forces, cannot now reflect this potential.

Since 1945, Asia has been the primary zone of world conflict but, in spite of this, a number of countries, and notably Japan, have followed deliberate policies of restraint in developing their military power. China, India, and Pakistan, the three strongest military powers of the area, are also the poorest in per capita terms; in each case the cost to society of modern capital-intensive forces is inordinately high. This has not discouraged their armament buildup in the past and there is no reason to believe that societal poverty will be an obstacle to further military outlays in the future. As in previous evaluations, only full-time military personnel are meant to be included in the base index of the manpower figures; in the case of the People's Republic of China a million troops have been added to the armed forces total as a rough approximation for the contribution of militia forces. While the "armed militia" has a manpower of several million, only a proportion of these part-time soldiers could operate in a military manner in field operations—except in the unlikely event of a foreign invasion in depth and military occupation, in which case many more could be engaged in a "People's War" against the enemy's administration (see Table VII).

TABLE VI
Non-Nuclear Military Forces:
Estimates of Equivalent Combat Capabilities

Mid-East and North Africa	Total Manpower (thousands)	Manpower Quality	Weapon Effectiveness	Infrastructure & Logistics	Organizational Quality	Average	Equivalent Units of Combat Capability
Israel	400	0.9	0.8	0.8	1	0.9	360
Egypt	343	0.3	0.6	0.3	0.4	0.4	137
Iran	300	0.2	0.5	0.3	0.2	0.3	90
Syria	227	0.3	0.6	0.3	0.3	0.4	91
Iraq	158	0.2	0.5	0.2	0.2	0.3	47
Sub-Saharan Africa							
Nigeria	230	0.1	0.1	0.1	0.2	0.1	23
South Africa	190	0.6	0.7	0.6	0.5	0.6	114

TABLE VII
Non-Nuclear Military Forces:
Estimates of Equivalent Combat Capabilities

Asia	Total Manpower (thousands)	Manpower Quality	Weapon Effectiveness	Infrastructure & Logistics	Organizational Quality	Average	Equivalent Units of Combat Capability
China (PRC)	4,525	0.4	0.2	0.2	0.3	0.3	1,357
India	1,055	0.2	0.4	0.3	0.3	0.3	317
Vietnam	615	0.5	0.4	0.3	0.9	0.5	308
South Korea	595	0.5	0.4	0.6	0.5	0.5	298
North Korea	495	0.4	0.6	0.6	0.5	0.5	248
China/Taiwan	470	0.6	0.5	0.6	0.6	0.6	282
Pakistan	428	0.3	0.4	0.2	0.3	0.3	128
Indonesia	246	0.2	0.1	0.2	0.1	0.2	49
Japan	235	0.8	0.6	0.7	0.8	0.7	165
Thailand	210	0.3	0.3	0.2	0.2	0.3	63
Burma	170	0.1	0.1	0.1	0.1	0.1	17
Afghanistan	100	0.2	0.2	0.1	0.1	0.2	20

Unlike economic power, or for that matter strategic-nuclear power, the capability of non-nuclear military forces wanes quite rapidly with distance. Armed forces which could be formidable on home ground, such as those of Switzerland, may have very little capability even a short distance beyond national borders. Mobility is a crucial attribute of military power and may absorb an important proportion of the total resources allocated to the armed forces. But mobility does not in itself define "strategic reach," which is a function of geographic position as well as of the long-range mobility of the armed forces concerned. Thus the Soviet Union had a great deal of strategic reach even in the days when its airlift and sealift capacities over long ranges were in fact very small. Already its vast territory gave access to both Europe and Northeast Asia. In fact, strategic reach is a function of three factors: geographic position, the mobility vehicles themselves, both sealift and airlift, and the whole complex of bases and forces which allows such airlift and sealift to be used in conflict situations. Thus in the American case a residual system of worldwide bases, the carrier task forces of the Navy, the entire Marine Corps, and the largest airlift capacity in the world combine to provide a unique degree of strategic reach.

Even for the United States, however, this does not mean that its full military strength can be successfully delivered anywhere in the world. Outside Europe and Northeast Asia where major U.S. forces are already pre-deployed, the global strategic reach of the United States amounts to the ability to deliver at short notice (30 days plus) up to one-and-a-third Marine divisions, and up to two (smaller) air-delivered Army divisions together with a commensurate amount of air power, but without the normal complement of armor. This is only a fraction of the total armed strength of the United States, but still very much more than any other country, including the Soviet Union, could deliver overseas. Moreover the United States has a major "forcible entry" capability in its amphibious assault Marine forces and its aircraft carriers, which can provide substantial air power over any coastal area of the world. Of course, even in the American case, a global strategic reach does not amount to global strategic access; there are already a good many places in Europe and Asia where even a four-carrier task force (300+ combat aircraft) cannot provide sufficient air power to suppress local air forces, and where even one-and-a-third Marine divisions cannot be landed with any hope of consolidating a beachhead.

Of course strategic reach does not have to be global in order to give international political significance to non-nuclear military capabilities employed in a local contest. For countries in regions of global importance, such as Western Europe, the Levant, or Northeast Asia, even a regional reach will count for a great deal in the arena of international politics. Hence in computing the final estimates of international military power in Table VIII below, variables reflecting strategic reach will be factored into the equation on the basis of politectonic positions as well as on that of mobility at sea and in the air. The conversion factor used here is designed to give value to the nation with the greatest reach—the United States—on a scale of perceived weight that has a maximum of 100, thus making it equivalent and comparable with nuclear forces capability and other elements of strength already analyzed in this calculus.

TABLE VIII
Net Total Non-Nuclear Military Power

Country	Equivalent Units of Combat Capability	Strategic Reach (0.01 to 0.05)	Net Total
United States	1,877	0.05	94
USSR	3,080	0.03	92
NATO & U.S. Allies			
West Germany (FRG)	464	0.03	14
France	359	0.03	11
United Kingdom	275	0.03	8
Turkey	245	0.03	7
Italy	181	0.03	5
Netherlands	90	0.03	3
Greece	100	0.02	2
Belgium	70	0.03	2
Canada	55	0.02	1
Denmark	21	0.03	1
Norway	27	0.03	1
Portugal	24	0.02	1
Spain	151	0.03	5
South Korea	298	0.02	6
Japan	165	0.03	5
China/Taiwan	282	0.02	6

Country	Equivalent Units of Combat Capability	Strategic Reach (0.01 to 0.05)	Net Total
Soviet Allies			
East Germany (GDR)	163	0.03	5
Czechoslovakia	133	0.03	4
Poland	180	0.02	4
Bulgaria	106	0.02	2
Hungary	84	0.02	2
Cuba	53	0.03	2
Rumania	96	0.01	1
Mideast and North Africa			
Israel	360	0.03	11
Egypt	137	0.03	4
Iran	90	0.03	3
Syria	91	0.02	2
Iraq	47	0.03	1
Sub-Saharan Africa			
South Africa	114	0.03	3
Nigeria	23	0.01	0.2
Latin America			
Brazil	77	0.02	2
Argentina	40	0.01	0.5
Asia			
China (PRC)	1,357	0.02	27
North Korea	248	0.03	7
India	317	0.01	3
Vietnam	308	0.01	3
Pakistan	128	0.01	1
Indonesia	49	0.02	1
Thailand	63	0.01	0.6
Burma	17	0.01	0.2
Afghanistan	20	0.01	0.2
European Neutrals			
Sweden	180	0.02	4
Yugoslavia	125	0.02	3
Switzerland	173	0.01	2

Scale of Military Effort

In view of the technical sophistication of the analysis of conventional military power employed in the preceding tables, reference to crude amounts of military expenditure adds little to an assessment of military capability. Still it is undeniable that perceptions of military power are influenced by the scale of national effort in terms of expenditures in support of military programs. It is commonplace in the United States to lament the comparatively low percentage of GNP devoted to military programs by Japan and the European NATO nations—on the grounds that they are not bearing a proportionate burden for common defense benefits.

On the contrary, some alarm has been aroused as a result of public release of the information that Soviet military expenditures have been recalculated by U.S. official intelligence experts at roughly 12 percent of GNP rather than a substantially lower percentage previously commonly accepted.[6] There was not much change in actual Soviet military weapons or forces involved in this new estimate, merely a change in cost analysis and methods of calculations; nevertheless, the perception of Soviet willingness to bear a heavy burden in support of expanding military programs has made an impression worldwide that magnifies perceptions of Soviet power.

Israel's extraordinary effort to maintain its defensive readiness, whereby its percentage of GNP devoted to military programs is the highest in the world, adds to the image of dynamic military capability it projects in the Mideast. Similarly the high rate of expenditure on arms by the Arab states neighboring Israel connotes a scale of military effort that adds to perceptions of danger of military conflict in the area. The perceptions are not altered too much by the fact that neither Israel nor Egypt and Syria could maintain their effort without massive support from the United States in the case of Israel or massive aid from the USSR and other Arab states on the opposing side. The net effort is an image of military capability above the norm.

Accordingly one more process of manipulating data reflecting military strength is the addition of bonus weights to those few nations with exceptionally high percentages of GNP devoted to bearing their military burdens. This factor is only relevant to nations with comparatively large armies and amounts only to a maximum of 10 in the scale of military capability we have employed whereby 100 is the maximum weight. Only Israel rates at the top of the scale. The natural breakpoint below which no bonus credit is given appears to be at about 8 percent of GNP, and there are not many nations with considerable armed forces that are making this level of effort. Most of the NATO nations spend less than 5 percent of GNP on military programs.

The United States showed what a modern industrial nation can do when it raised its 2 percent of GNP for military effort during the 1930s era of neutrality and isolation to a peak of 48 percent in 1944 in order to win World War II. This effort ended with the U.S. economy vibrant, dynamic, and innovative at a time when most other economies were in ruins, and in a sense U.S. strategic domination of world affairs in the postwar quarter-century is based on this extraordinary scale of military effort in World War II. The United States immediately cut its programs back sharply as it entered the postwar era and has never exceeded the 12 percent of GNP level reached during the Korean War in the early 1950s. At the maximum period of U.S. alliance building efforts in 1956, U.S. military expenditures amounted to 9.3 percent of GNP; they dropped to 8.3 percent just before heavy involvement in the Vietnam war, reached a peak of 9.4 percent of GNP in 1968 and have since fallen back to the mid-1970s level of between 5 percent and 6 percent—something like the world average for military spending.[7] It is for this reason that no bonus can be given to the United States for military effort in comparison to economic strength and that a number of other nations deserve additional weights to indicate the perception of extraordinary effort they make to increase their military capability.

The following nations are assigned bonus weights for perceived military power;[8] the USSR projects the greatest image of military dynamism, of course, because a percentage point of its vast GNP looms larger in real and psychological terms than the others:

Country	Percent of GNP	Bonus Weight	Net Total Weight
USSR	12	5	97
Israel	35	10	21
Vietnam	22	5	8
Iran	15	5	8
Iraq	15	5	6
Syria	12	5	7
Egypt	11	5	9
China (PRC)	11	5	32
North Korea	10	5	12
China/Taiwan	9	5	11

With these adjustments our assessment of nations perceived as having military capabilities constituting leverage in international affairs is complete. The crude measurement it provides is summarized along with the other elements of national power evaluated up to this point in our study in the next chapter.

CHAPTER SIX

Summary of the Concrete Elements of Power: $P_p = (C + E + M) \times (S + W)$

Thus far in our calculus of the attributes and distribution of national power as perceived in international affairs, we have been dealing with relatively concrete elements of power. They are at least somewhat quantifiable, even though perceptions of such broad national characteristics are bound to be impressionistic to a certain degree. At this point, the maximum total of perceived power weights any single nation could possess is 500.[1] The United States comes close to this total because in fact it stands at the top, or close to the top, of almost every ranklist and tends to set the standard for maximum feasible achievement. There is nothing foreordained about this phenomenon; things were quite different 50 years ago and it is difficult to predict the future more than five or ten years ahead. For the present, however, the United States is clearly the front runner, in having most of the concrete elements of power. The range of variation below the maximum standard is great. The total of perceived power weights for each of the additional countries that are taken into consideration for one reason or another falls off sharply from the top rankings. The nations that project an image of great power at this point in history are not very numerous, and the many countries at the third and fourth levels of national power register comparatively very low in our calculus.

After consideration of economic, strategic–nuclear, and conventional military capability (Chapters Three, Four, and Five), we are now able to add all these concrete value weights to the consolidated ranklist of nations with considerable perceived power. It is also necessary to adjust the order in which nations are listed to reflect perceived power in all categories: population and territory (critical mass), economic capability, and military capability. The resulting consolidated list is as follows:

Total Macrometric Power Pattern: C + E + M (by zones)

Zone	Country	Critical Mass	Economic Weight	Strategic Weapons	Conventional Military	Total	Total for Politectonic Zones
I	United States	100	174	100	94	468	
	Canada	70	26		1	97	641
	Mexico	70	4			74	
	Jamaica		2			2	
II	USSR	100	105	100	97	402	
	Poland	35	9		4	48	
	Mongolia	30				30	
	Rumania	20	3		1	24	
	East Germany (GDR)	10	7		5	22	546
	Czechoslovakia		6		4	10	
	Hungary		3		2	5	
	Bulgaria		1		2	3	
	Cuba				2	2	
III	PRC	100	29	10	32	171	
	Vietnam	40			8	48	241
	North Korea	10			12	22	

West Germany (FRG)	50	48		14	112
France	55	36		11	112
United Kingdom	55	26	10	8	99
Italy	50	16	10	5	71
Spain	45	9		5	59
Yugoslavia	30	3		3	36
Sweden	15	10		4	29
Norway	15	4		1	20
IV Finland	15	2			17
Netherlands		12		3	15
Belgium		10		2	12
Switzerland		6		2	8
Denmark		4		1	5
Austria		4			4
Greece		1		2	3
Portugal		1		1	2
Albania		1			1
					605

Zone	Country	Critical Mass	Economic Weight	Strategic Weapons	Conventional Military	Total	Total for Politectonic Zones
	Iran	60	12		8	80	
	Egypt	55	1		9	65	
	Turkey	55	3		7	65	
	Saudi Arabia	30	13			43	
	Algeria	40	1			41	
	Sudan	40				40	
V	Libya	30	3			33	457
	Morocco	30				30	
	Iraq	15	4		6	25	
	Israel		1		21	22	
	Syria				7	7	
	Kuwait		4			4	
	UAE		2			2	
	India	90	4		3	97	
VI	Pakistan	60	1		1	62	229
	Bangladesh	40				40	
	Afghanistan	30				30	
	Indonesia	80	4		1	85	
	Burma	50				50	
VII	Thailand	45	1		1	47	224
	Philippines	40	1			41	
	Singapore		1			1	

Zone	Nation					
VIII	Japan	60	46	5	111	
	South Korea	30	2	6	38	172
	China/Taiwan	10	2	11	23	
IX	Brazil	85	7	2	94	
	Argentina	65	5	1	71	
	Colombia	40	1		41	
	Peru	30	1		31	
	Venezuela	20	6		26	
	Chile	20	2		22	
	Guyana		1		1	
	Surinam		1		1	287
X	Nigeria	60	5		65	
	South Africa	50	7	3	60	
	Zaire	55			55	
	Ethiopia	45			45	
	Tanzania	30			30	
	Zambia	20	2		22	
	Rhodesia	15	1		16	
	Guinea	10	2		12	305
XI	Australia	40	20		60	
	New Zealand	10	1		11	71

TOTAL FOR ALL ZONES (76 nations)   3,778

This comprehensive consolidated ranklist indicates that 76 nations have some claim to significant power on the basis of our calculus. In some cases it is a claim based on a single valuable asset supported by little else in the way of strength. For example, Kuwait has only one economic asset, oil; Guinea, bauxite.

Apparent anomalies in the ranklist can be explained; it must be remembered that each country is an individual case. Cuba, with limited national strength except for the military programs made possible by its status as the only Soviet client state in the western hemisphere, has had a great deal of impact on international affairs because of its highly visible military troublemaking potential, especially in providing proxy armed forces to assist pro-Soviet political groups in seizing control in strife-torn Angola. Similarly, Syria, Israel's Arab neighbor possessing military might rather than oil, received a great deal of international attention and prestige as a result of moving its armies into Lebanon to end the complex civil strife there and, in effect, to occupy most of the country.

In all, these 76 nations include over 85 percent of the peoples of the world and all of the powerful nations. Among them, 50 or so overshadow the rest, and what happens to these leading nations will determine the trends in world power over the next 10 to 20 years.

The real advantage of a consolidated ranklist of this kind is to focus attention on the concentration of great power in the hands of a relatively small number of leading nations and to observe how this power is distributed geographically. The total number of weighted values, that is, units of perceived power in this macrometric pattern of international affairs, is 3,778. The United States and the USSR alone have 870, which demonstrates once again that it is still to a surprising degree a biploar world we live in; the next most powerful nations are only about one-quarter to one-third as strong as these two superpowers. On the basis of the macrometric analysis we have considered so far, these 76 nations, less than one-half of those in the world, are the ones that will tend to figure in international affairs.

This listing permits us to turn to our next task, the attempt to consider political and strategic factors in looking at these countries and zones. North America is overwhelming insofar as the three large nations cooperate; the bauxite of Jamaica is just an extra fillip. Obviously, Soviet domination of bordering nations is a useful increment of strength even though Mongolia is important only in the Sino-Soviet context and

Rumania is an unreliable asset for the USSR and its allies, since it is invariably the holdout for independence within the Warsaw Pact.

The PRC looms over East Asia as a result of size alone. Hanoi's victory is too recent for it to affect the real power factors of 1977 very much, although strategically it is politically more important than North Korea, the other Asian Communist nation. A period of organization and regimentation is inevitable before control of the population and territory of South Vietnam can be mobilized for Hanoi's strategic benefit in its dealings with Southeast Asia. It will, in due time, be a power to be reckoned with in regional terms.

Indonesia's strategic position commanding the Malacca Straits—along with Singapore—and other passageways between the southwest Pacific and Indian Oceans, makes the whole area of Southeast Asia a focal point of great power interest. For some time to come the states of Zone VII will be potential trouble spots inviting fragmentation, conflict, and national jockeying for influence.

The clear message for West Europe from our evaluation is that it could be one of the most powerful regional centers in the world if its power potential were successfully mobilized for a common political purpose. Since this is not now the case, the crucial question is whether West Europe becomes simply a rich prize for conflicting superpowers in a strategically Finlandized—i.e., neutralized—region or whether the 25-year-old Atlantic Alliance will cohere sufficiently to make the two power centers in it (West Europe and North America) count as one strategic bloc internationally.

The political fragmentation of the Mideast, South Asia, and Northeast Asia shows how these regions run the risk of being dominated by better organized nations or alliances even though they are potentially very powerful in themselves. For example, the strategic triangle of countries in Northeast Asia—Japan, China/Taiwan, and South Korea—appears to be collectively capable of counterbalancing the still limited strength of Communist China only if the United States insures their strategic coherence through bilateral relations with all three, to compensate for their limited political cooperation with one another.

The same problems explain why Central and Southern Africa, on the one hand, and Latin America, on the other, are only beginning to develop as great regional power centers. The natural focal points in both of these continental regions are mutually antagonistic, politically and strategically, e.g., Brazil vis-à-vis Argentina and Nigeria vis-à-vis South Africa.

137

Plainly Mongolia—locked between China and the Asian USSR—and Cuba—in the western hemisphere—are in some contexts additions of strength but in others more like potential conflict areas inside other zones. China's relations with North Korea are shaky and its political foothold in Southeast Europe, Albania, is more liability than asset except in the sphere of Communist ideology.

In West Europe, neutral Sweden and policy-straitjacketed Finland may indicate the wave of the future for the NATO powers rather than adding incremental strength. The USSR views Finland as the "model for the development of relations" with the rest of West Europe.[2] Yugoslavia tries desperately to stay nonaligned between the Soviet bloc and West Europe, although it will have difficulty in doing so after Tito's death.

In the Mideast, Israel exists among the Arab states in an equilibrium of military tension which has been and can again be shattered by war. The potentially crushing superiority of Arab-Islamic strength in this zone is clear. Elsewhere diversity and disunity are the common rule, except in Zone XI, where New Zealand's strength combined with that of Australia creates a fairly homogenous cluster of peoples of European origin in the Outer Ocean perimeter. Even here, however, the whole zone is vulnerable in view of the comparatively small population residing in it and the disorder among the nations in neighboring Zone VII, Southeast Asia.

It is to reduce this chaotic picture to some semblance of order for purposes of strategic analysis that we have employed the concept of leading nations in the several zones. This clarity, gained by simplification, does not alter the fact that each politectonic zone has its own regional character, plus those anomalies in the distribution of power of the kind listed above.

There is one more useful way to look at the distribution of power among these 76 nations which register on the scale of international power according to our calculus. It is to classify politectonic zones on a broad political spectrum. Zones II and III contain the totalitarian states with closed societies and command economies. About 35 percent of the world's population lives in these zones, most of it being Chinese, but the total perceived macrometric power of nations in Zone II and Zone III is only about 20 percent of the world total as we have calculated it. Zone I,

North America, and Zone IV, West Europe, are comparatively small but they add up to about one-third of the world total of perceived macrometric power. The United States, in combination with only the closest U.S. allies in other zones, possesses a preponderance of power as perceived according to the macrometric factors so far considered. The open societies and economies with substantial private enterprise and world trade are collectively very strong. Superficial examination of their share of world power suggests they should feel secure, not endangered.

Yet the fall of South Vietnam in 1975 marked a major shift away from U.S. influence and economic access at the fractured edge of one of the politectonic zones. The shock waves have made a deep global impression. Perceptions of power have changed in the United States and abroad. This expulsion of U.S. power is the intended Chinese and North Vietnamese pattern for conflicts of the future.

If revolution or war brings a similar strategic movement away from the United States and its allies in the Mideast, a tremendous shift in politectonic structure would ensue. To put the matter simply, the USSR is engaged in a long-term effort to gain sufficient political influence over parts of the Mideast to endanger access by the international free market economies to its valuable economic resource, oil. Soviet leaders feel that to create disorder in the area is to their advantage even if they do not immediately gain control. Since Mideast oil is crucial to economic and socio-political stability in West Europe and Japan for the next decade, to say nothing of being financially unsettling for the United States, such a gain for the USSR would result in economic insecurity for the trading nations of the northern hemisphere. Such political and economic turmoil would entail a crucial shift in the comparative "correlation of forces" and a fracturing of key politectonic zones. In the strategic tensions of the Mideast and pressures toward Finlandization in West Europe, we see the preferred pattern Moscow envisages for confrontations under the conditions of detente.

Because of instabilities inherent in the present distribution of world power, it is essential to move on to political and strategic factors that affect the strength of nations and also to look at clusters of powers associated or allied within and across the borders of the politectonic zones. These considerations constitute the subject matter of our closing chapters. Since our focus is on global strategy as a factor in the international balance of power, we will mainly deal in this context with the top ranking nations, the USSR, the United States, and China, each of which has a view of the way it would like the world to develop.

CHAPTER SEVEN

National Strategy and National Will:
$P_p = (C + E + M) \times (S + W)$

A ll of the macrometric calculations reflected in the foregoing chapters provide a rough guide to the focal power points in the world today. From the beginning, however, we have indicated that our results would be modified by an estimate of the effectiveness of national strategies and national will.

It is crucial to note that the formula calls for a coefficient, a multiplier, reflecting these two factors, S and W. While earlier elements of power have been treated as roughly additive, the use of a multiplication sign in the formula at this point means that the value of the whole equation can be substantially altered by the factors that constitute the coefficient that comes after it. This is bound to be true because anything multiplied by zero equals zero. Thus substantial concrete elements of power may be reduced to nearly nothing if a coherent national strategy is lacking or if there is little organized national political will to carry out any strategy.

As we now have rough quantifications for C + E + M, we can complete our assessment if we factor in the right coefficient to reflect the last part of the equation: $P_p = (C + E + M) \times (S + W)$.

People join together in a nation because they share common purposes over and above their individual goals in life. Not everyone in a nation need agree on all those broader purposes, but there is a general direction or trend discernible in every community, whether or not it is clearly articulated. Most national goals concern such domestic issues as the distribution of wealth among citizens and the balance between authority and civil order on the one hand, and protection for individual and minority rights, on the other.

In international affairs, the common purpose of a nation ought to include a general strategy for dealing with other nations in ways that protect and enhance the agreed goals of the citizenry, as represented by the government leaders entrusted with responsibility for foreign policy. Though defense departments define military policies and foreign offices elaborate diplomatic positions, the bedrock foundations of foreign policy must be the political aspirations and moral concepts of the people as expressed through their representatives at the national level. Strategy may sometimes be only a pattern of behavior reflecting cultural norms; at other times, most especially in wartime, it is carefully articulated. In a dictatorship, policies can be worked out with precision and made mandatory. The range of possible international strategies runs from a total isolation from the affairs of other nations (Japan in the early nineteenth century) to carefully plotted campaigns of territorial conquest (Germany under Hitler). Even when spelled out only vaguely in most citizens' minds, national policies determine the conditions for cooperation or conflict with other countries and hence, in extreme cases, the chances for political life or death—for national survival or extinction.

Here we enter a region where numbers can only be notations of highly subjective judgments, nothing more. Yet the judgments are critical and must be made, even though reasonable men will inevitably differ on them. The task is simplified to some extent if it is recognized at the outset that most nations have only local or limited aims and are largely passive observers of strategic measures on a global scale. Powerful nations with broad international interests need a global strategy to focus their energies. Secondary and tertiary powers fashion their national policies in accordance with the associations they have formed with more powerful nations. In this situation the easiest way to deal with most countries is to assume that normally they are preoccupied with local and regional interests, but that they can summon up sufficient political and social cohesion to pursue their rather limited national purposes with reasonable effectiveness in the international arena if the need arises. Their national strategies are largely protective, i.e., defensive, and their national will is usually tested only in the relatively easy context of domestic self-defense.

In such cases, the index weight will be 1, or normal, for combined strategic purpose (S) and national will (W); that is, 0.5 for strategy and 0.5 for will. If the multiplier is 1, the value of the rest of the formula is unchanged. It is an arbitrary scale of measurement but it has the advantage of leaving most numerical weights unchanged, while focusing on deviations above and below the normal, i.e., the expected behavior pattern. In fact we will concentrate only on those nations that by the standards of the more concrete elements of power are perceived as major movers and shakers in the world arena.

In the case of nations with clear-cut strategic plans for international aggrandizement, a larger index number for the factor S may be assigned, up to an arbitrary maximum of 1. If, similarly, nations are unified socially, psychologically, and politically behind strategic aims, they also may be assigned a larger index number for the factor W, up to an arbitrary maximum of 1. Thus a maximum score would result in a multiplier of 2 for the term combining S and W. Other elements of national strength would be correspondingly magnified. In this way the total feasible score becomes twice the sum of the concrete elements of power summarized in the last chapter. The maximum total of 500 perceived power weights theoretically could be increased to 1,000, although it is unlikely any real nation would make so high a score. In fact, many nations fall below the normal level of 1 for their strategy and national will.

If a nation is strategically confused and its will to pursue a policy is feeble, it may get a fractional index rating below 0.5 for one or for both of these more intangible factors. In that case the values for other elements of national power would be reduced. In an extreme hypothetical case, a zero multiplier would give a zero quantity of perceived power, regardless of other potential strengths that may exist; as pointed out above, anything times nothing is nothing. A large and powerful nation with no strategy at all and no will whatsoever could hardly exist, but at various times even the greatest of nations suffer from a confusion of strategic purpose or a weakening of national will. Hence the multiplier can be considerably less than the normal index score of 1.

This calculation is critical in the whole analysis of perceptions of world power. In the exercise of great power, standards must be rigorous because the competition is severe. Hence any falling off by one of the large and potentially powerful nations in these crucial matters of strategy and of strength of will is a severe handicap in the use of power for international purposes. Factoring in these final, intangible elements of national strength therefore becomes the most important part of any net assessment of the international balance of power.

The final result of the application of this methodology is that the concrete elements of national power (population, territory, economic capability, and military capability) theoretically could be doubled or reduced nearly to zero, as the result of consideration of the less tangible qualities of strategic purpose and political will.

Only three nations in the recent past have had an integrated, truly global strategic concept in the conduct of their international affairs. They are the USSR, the United States, and the People's Republic of China. These are, of course, very large countries with tremendous strengths.

Other dynamic powers with positive strategic programs in the period prior to World War II were Germany and Japan, on the one hand, with France and the United Kingdom resisting them, on the other. All four were nearly destroyed in the struggle and their strategic purpose over the past 30 years has mainly been to regain strength and to reconstruct beneficial protective alliances. It is a remarkable fact of twentieth century history that the foes of the United States in World War II have become its close allies. This phenomenon is due to an extraordinarily generous American postwar occupation policy and to the healthy defensive reaction of Germany and Japan to the crude and disruptive pressures brought to bear on them by the USSR.

Other nations for the most part orient themselves around—or against—the very large and powerful countries, or in economic, political, and military combinations related to the three very large nations—the USSR, the United States, and China—or the four renascent secondary powers, Germany, Japan, the United Kingdom, and France. Regional associations of nations and groups dedicated to "nonalignment" with any of the great powers have also been formed, especially in Asia and Africa, but their exercise of influence in world affairs is limited—limited largely to propaganda and the weary wars of words at the United Nations. In 1977 several newer nations of consequence, like Iran and Brazil, are thrusting themselves into the ranks of the globally involved powers, but in discussing international strategy the field remains comparatively small.

144

National Will

A nation may be either efficient or inept in carrying out its policies, depending on the strength of the political will of the people as expressed in their national decision-making. National will may be unified and enthusiastic in support of a particular strategy or it may be sluggish and uncertain. The degree of energy and coherent behavior in a body politic is the main cause of its success or failure. Still, firmness of national will depends in part on whether strategic aims have been wisely formulated and skillfully explained in terms of national interest. This explanatory function is crucial in a representative government based on the consent of the governed.

To have a reasonable and defensible basis for quantifying the national will of the countries of the world, we must begin by closely scrutinizing the identifiable elements which comprise nationhood: how people of a country perceive themselves in relation to each other as well as to the world around them, and how their society provides modes and procedures for acting upon these perceptions. These are the elements of national life which require analysis in order better to understand the phenomenon we are trying to pin down with a numerical rating.

National will is the quality which enables a nation to bring its resources and capabilities effectively to bear for a perceived national purpose, the nation's strategy. It is not a fixed quality of unchanging value; in fact it is ephemeral, fluctuating. The degree to which attitudes, values, and purposes are shared in a nation affects the strength of its will. But even more important is the character of the national leadership and, more particularly, the authority that leadership possesses to act, an authority which may have been bestowed by established tradition or popularly chosen governmental organization, or may have been obtained by force. No matter how achieved, the authority to act has limits and rests ultimately on the reaction of the people toward both the leadership and the stated national strategy.

The elements of national will are multiple and diverse; no one element seems to be an absolute requisite for national strength of purpose. If a common language appears essential, then one looks to Switzerland where multilingualism seems to be no impediment to unity. If ethnic uniformity appears to be vital, then one finds that great ethnic diversity has been largely surmounted and in a sense is a strengthening factor in the United States. Indeed, it seems that each nation offers an almost unique combination of those individual elements which establish the degree of unity and strength of will which that nation possesses.

Amidst this diversity, however, certain elements repeatedly emerge in contributory strands in the fabric of national will.[1] For further discussion and analysis those elements can be grouped as follows:

1. Level or degree of cultural integration of the people in a feeling of belonging to a nation.
2. Effective strength of national leadership.
3. Relevance of national strategy to national interests as they are perceived by the citizens.

Level of National Integration

From the extensive research that has been undertaken in our times on nationalism and the process of national integration, two factors are repeatedly identified as most significant, first, cultural uniformity, and second, the concept of national territoriality.

The chief components of cultural uniformity are: ethnicity, language, and religion. The degree of uniformity in each determines the contribution each makes to national integration. Perfect uniformity is not required but the level of integration a nation achieves can be perceived in part—and measured—by the relative contribution of each component.

Where diversity exists, whether that diversity is in plural ethnic backgrounds, multiple languages, or different religions, successfully integrated nations seem to make specific adjustments to accommodate this diversity. Yugoslavia and Switzerland, for example, comprise many nations, i.e., ethnic groups "bound together in a single political and territorial unit by feelings of patriotism derived from ideology, memories of a common struggle against external or alien powers, and rational calculations of common advantage in the sharing of a single political structure."[2] Similar adjustments are also made to accommodate diversity in language and religion. Uniformity is not essential to nationhood in either of these powerful cultural factors, and each apparently can replace the other as a dominant force in integration. India provides a good example:

> Language in north India has generally played a secondary role to religion as a source of social and political differentiation. Yet it would not be correct to conclude . . . that religion is inherently a more powerful motive force in identity formation than language because elsewhere in the world, and in India itself, the roles of these two forces have been reversed. In south India, in Europe, and in Africa, it has been more common for language to provide a basis for nationalism in religiously diverse societies whereas, in north India, religion has united linguistically distinct peoples, particularly the Muslims.[3]

Another important component in the level or degree of integration of the people in a nation is the regard which the people have for their historical heritage, their collective memory of an often greatly idealized past. In examining the role of history and legend in the emerging nationality of the United States, a distinguished American historian explains:

> Local loyalties and local prejudices became only gradually submerged to become part of a national patriotism. Much of this derived from the creation of American folk heroes—i.e., Davy Crockett, George Washington—and from the joint effort to gain independence from the British, as seen and remembered in retrospect.[4]

Jawaharlal Nehru, himself now well along in the process of becoming a national folk hero, described his efforts in India shortly after independence had been achieved from the British to make the peasants "think of India as a whole."

> The task was not easy; yet it was not so difficult as I had imagined, for our ancient epics and myth and legend, which they knew so well, had made them familiar with the conception of their country.[5]

If the people who occupy a geographic area are to be fused into a nation it is essential for those people to have a feeling of belonging to a still larger or more abstract entity, their country. The stronger the psychological conviction is among the people that their own village is one of many dots on a national map, the greater will be the contribution this concept of national territoriality makes to integration. If the citizens look outside their local environs to an unseen larger community of which they feel a part, they are on the path to nationhood.

In general, the longer a country has retained its essential geographic outline, the stronger a sense of territoriality becomes in the minds of its inhabitants. As the years become decades and the decades, centuries, people progressively regard the surrounding countryside as only an extension of their own homesteads. This process is furthered by a growing awareness that the neighbors over the hill, or in the next province, have over the years joined in such national emergencies as fighting a war or combatting a flood.

In some nations, however, this process has not been completed; it appears arrested by the greater prominence of, or greater loyalty accorded to, territorial entities within the nation. All countries of any size have a degree of regionalism; in some, it is strong enough to weaken significantly the concept of national territoriality. This is most likely to be true when geographic regionalism is reinforced by cultural diversity, especially language or religion. The USSR has a special weakness in the great variety of separate national identities within its vast sweep of territory. In most well-integrated nations the element of regionalism is subordinated to the national concept, especially when the nation confronts a substantial challenge.

The majority of the world's nations occupy geographic territory which is contiguous throughout and have within their national boundaries considerable uniformity of terrain and climate. Where the land is not contiguous, and where the geographic features are greatly dissimilar from one region to another, the concept of national territoriality is to some degree weakened. The people of Indonesia, who occupy an archipelago which extends for 1,500 miles between the Indian and Pacific Oceans, encounter greater difficulty in thinking of themselves as part of a single geographic whole than do the people of Poland. The people of Colombia, where part of the population lives in a temperate zone at a 7,000-foot altitude and where another part lives in a tropical climate at sea level, have a similar difficulty.

To recapitulate what has been suggested regarding those elements which determine the level of national integration, there can be said to be two major components: 1) the degree of cultural uniformity, and 2) the strength of the concept of national territoriality. Besides these, two other qualities figure significantly in shaping the strength of a nation's will: the effective caliber of its national leadership and the perceived relevance of the national strategy to the national interest.

Strength of National Leadership

The two chief elements which determine the effective strength of national leadership appear to be: 1) the capacity of the country's governmental system to formulate, elucidate, and implement a national strategy, and 2) the normal response level of the populace, which may range from apathetic to enthusiastic.

One can judge the capacity of a government to make national strategy only by direct observation of each nation at work. There are no generalizations which will apply everywhere, although it is generally true that simple monarchies, dictatorships, and ideologically-directed nations tend to function more effectively in a primitive psychological sense in this area than democracies. Of greater significance than the theoretical structure of a government is the level of expectation it has established that an enunciation of policy will command respect and elicit response. Japan is an example of a country where enunciated policy has nearly always received a positive response.

At the other extreme are nations such as those in South Asia that have been characterized as "soft states." In these,

> There is an unwillingness among the rulers to impose obligations on the governed and a corresponding unwillingness on their part to obey rules laid down by democratic procedures. The tendency is to use the carrot, not the stick. The level of social discipline is low compared with all Western countries—not to mention Communist countries.[6]

In this statement the noted sociologist, Gunnar Myrdal, sets forth by implication the two chief elements in effective leadership: government decisiveness in establishing policy and the response norm—the social discipline—of the populace. Between the two extremes noted in the leadership equation—Japan and, say, Sri Lanka—lie most of the countries in the world.

Perceived Relevance of National Strategy to National Interest

Because national will is ultimately the expression of the aggregate emotions and desires of a people, it is essentially a human response we are measuring, and human beings respond with greater intensity to some situations than to others. A national strategy evokes a level of response appropriate to the degree of national interest—that is, the aggregate of perceived individual interests—it represents to the populace. Probably the highest level of national interest is evoked by a strategy which is perceived to be directed toward national self-protection or survival. A vivid example is the stand made in 1941 by the Russian people against the invading Germans, a response which sharply contrasts with their restrained enthusiasm for achieving the Politburo's assigned agricultural norms.

Other national strategies may be perceived by the population as considerably less closely related to the national interest and therefore less likely to evoke a positive response. A strategy which seems to be concerned largely with aggrandizing the personal glory of the leadership, or which seeks mainly to elevate a minority group to a higher social or economic position, would clearly be less energizing to the populace as a whole. But in between these extremes lies an infinite variety of possible strategies about which it is impossible to speak categorically. There are, to be sure, certain constants. Any national strategy which succeeds in enhancing the economic well-being of the majority of the population can be assured of some degree of positive response. Likewise, a strategy which seeks to achieve a superior position over an established enemy, whether by economic competition or force of arms, can expect strong support from the people. Perhaps even broader responsive effort comes from a strategy of preventing an established national enemy from achieving a superior position over one's own country; at least this is likely if the danger of being out-distanced in the contest for power is clearly seen by the people as well as the leaders of a nation. Whatever the strategy chosen by the leadership, its perceived relevance to the aggregate interests of the people will be a significant factor in determining the response and support it receives.

Quantitative Values in Assessing National Will

It is necessary to turn now to the uncertain task of quantifying the separate elements which together create the strength of a nation's will. This task is if anything more difficult and more susceptible to subjective judgment than was the effort to quantify national strategies. Yet such an attempt can be useful and can illuminate the discussion even though other observers would prefer to use different values.

In assigning values to the various elements we have isolated as contributing to the strength of a nation's will, it appears that approximately equal weight ought to be given to the three main groupings—national integration, strength of leadership, and relevance of strategy. Our allocation of values within the three groupings, based on their relative importance in national will, would then be:

1. Level of national integration
   a. Cultural integration...25%
   b. Territorial integration.......................................8%

2. Strength of national leadership
   a. Governmental policy capability.........................17%
   b. Level of social discipline.................................17%

3. Relevance of strategy to national interest 33%

It should be noted that the percentages suggested are for the several components of national will, and that in summing them up we are continuing to work within our overall formula in which an index weight of 1 would be the maximum rating on national will, and a rating of 50 percent or 0.5 constitutes the normal or average. Few nations come even close to the maximum of 1 and many nations rate well below the norm of 0.5. Thus in our equation, $P_p = (C + E + M) \times (S + W)$, S and W combined constitute a coefficient of 1 as normal, more for exceptional clarity of strategy or strength of will, and less if a nation is deficient in these characteristics.

Soviet Strategy in a Global Perspective

Soviet strategic thinking reflects a consistent view of the evolving world situation—what Soviet ideologues call the "correlation of forces"—and a consistent operational code of international conduct designed to advance the interests of the Soviet Union within the constraints other nations impose on Soviet tactics and timing. Occasionally there are variations of language and tactics, but Soviet strategy has remained the same for a long time. At present, Soviet officials repeatedly explain that they are following a policy of "detente," but this term can only be understood in the context of general Soviet political thinking about "peaceful coexistence" with capitalism.

Soviet strategy in all its basic features was formulated by Lenin and Stalin, although Khrushchev and Brezhnev have naturally adjusted some features of it to fit new conditions. Still, Brezhnev's detente is essentially Lenin's peaceful coexistence. It is fashionable to discount all formulations of national goals as rhetoric or ideology, but in the case of a tightly organized dictatorship the pronouncements of national leaders set the norms for acceptable thinking and behavior on the part of the dutiful bureaucratic managers of society. Whether they are "true believers" is not too relevant since they are obliged in a command system of politics and economics to act on the strategic premises that have been officially established. The central thrust of Soviet policy is remarkably clear for those who read and listen, and it must be reckoned with by all who deal with the USSR.

Soviet leaders have always espoused the right to fight a "just war" of "national liberation," that is, to assist a country in shaking off external domination, as they would have said they were doing in Vietnam. Beyond that they have made it painfully clear, especially for the benefit of their own citizenry, that peaceful coexistence, in addition to avoiding total war, means (1) unrelenting class struggle; (2) worldwide support of the forces of revolution by the ballot if possible and by violence if necessary; (3) diplomatic moves to bring about political realignments in non-Communist areas so as to restrict the parts of the world open to U.S. influence, trade, investment, and procurement of economic raw materials;[7] and (4) permanent positive antipathy between the Communist and capitalist social systems, the latter of which, according to Soviet doctrine, is still supposed to perish in the ultimate and long-heralded "world crisis of capitalism."

Soviet statements for the past several years have carefully restricted the meaning of peaceful coexistence to fit this classical Marxist-Leninist theory of social conflict. Their purpose is to preserve and strengthen the one-party dictatorship in the Soviet Union, which insists on the total compliance of Soviet officials and the Soviet citizenry with doctrinal edicts on international strategy as well as with day-to-day administrative commands of the totalitarian government.

The clearest theoretical pronouncement on Soviet world strategy came from Stalin in "Economic Problems of Socialism in the USSR" shortly before his death in March 1953:

> The disintegration of a single universal world market must be considered the most important economic consequence of the Second World War. . . . This circumstance determined the further aggravation of the general crisis in the world capialist system. . . . It follows . . . that the sphere of exploitation of world resources by the major capitalist countries (USA, Britain, France) will not expand but contract, that the world market conditions will deteriorate for these countries and that the number of enterprises operating at less than capacity will multiply in these countries. It is this essentially which constitutes the aggravation of the general crisis in the world capitalist system due to disintegration of the world market.

Since the mid-1950s, under Khrushchev's leadership, military assistance and economic aid on a massive scale to countries which the USSR hoped could be won away from economic and political relations with the United States or West European "capitalist" powers have poured out in a mighty flood. While not quite so generous or ebullient as Khrushchev, Brezhnev has continued to use arms and money to gain influence over peripheral areas and to deny them to the West. Particularly in the Mideast, Soviet policy has brought a major change in the patterns of stability in this region and jeopardized the access of the United States, West Europe, and Japan to the oil which is vital to their industries.

Moscow's official newspaper, *Pravda,* said flatly in August 1973, after the touted summits held in Moscow and Washington:

> Peaceful coexistence does not mean the end of the struggle of the two-world social systems. The struggle between the proletariat and the bourgeoisie, between world socialism and imperialism, will be

waged right up to the complete and final victory of communism on a world scale.

There is a relentless consistency and clarity in Soviet thought about supporting revolutionary class warfare against non-Communist governments and aiding national wars of liberation from "imperialist," i.e., U.S., influence, as the "correlation of forces" in the world shifts in favor of the USSR. An international atmosphere of peaceful coexistence is understood by every Marxist-Leninist student to contribute to the conditions in which conflict remains below the dangerous intensity of total war and yet weakens capitalism, i.e., the United States and its allies, and strengthens the USSR.

These ideological concepts are taught throughout the USSR and they constitute part of the furniture in the minds of those Soviet leaders in the Communist Party bureaucracy who control foreign policy and make all strategic decisions. Brezhnev and his most influential colleagues in the Soviet Politburo are the last legatees of the grim decades of brutal Stalinist rule, most of them in their late sixties or early seventies. Some years hence younger men may modify the ideas and policies jealously nurtured by party officialdom for 60 years, but for the present and foreseeable future the best clue there is to Soviet international behavior is likely to be the same national strategy of fundamental and irreconcilable hostility toward leading non-Communist societies, particularly the strongest, the United States. By this simple strategic posture of opposition to U.S. international ties and interests the leaders of the USSR say they expect history to bring them ultimately to a position of strategic superiority over the United States, not in a narrow military sense but in the broader context of exercising superior influence over other lesser nations whose economic resources and technology enormously benefit whichever trading system—Soviet or U.S.—they belong to.

All good Communists are taught to believe that, as Mao Tse-tung proclaimed, "political power grows out of the barrel of a gun."[8] Soviet national strategy is simple and clear: to increase the relative power of the USSR in every sphere. At home it calls for steadily growing economic and military capabilities; internationally it operates by encouraging "class warfare" in all capitalist societies, thus weakening them, and by giving aid in "wars of national liberation"—i.e., limited wars to break political and economic links between the United States and smaller non-Communist nations where internal political "struggle" has a chance of ending up in the seizure of power by a pro-Soviet dictatorship. In this way, gradually, more and more of the peoples and economic resources of the globe become exploitable to the benefit of the USSR, or at least separated from the United States and its international trading bloc and security system of alliances.

Soviet leaders, whatever their private misgivings and realistic reservations, project an image of extraordinary confidence and conviction in speaking of Soviet long-range strategic goals and the trend of international events. The preeminent Old Bolshevik theoretician, Suslov, gave the Lenin Anniversary address at the April 16, 1975, meeting of the Central Committee of the Communist Party of the Soviet Union in Moscow, stressing the theme that:

> Under the conditions of detente and the further intensification of the general crisis of capitalism, the role of the international Communist movement as the most influential and active political force of our time is increasing.

Party General Secretary Brezhnev sounded the same note in the following excerpts from his triumphant speech to the Twenty-Fifth Party Congress in Moscow, February 24, 1976:

> No impartial person can deny that the socialist countries' influence on world affairs is becoming ever stronger and deeper.
>
> Our party supports and will continue to support peoples fighting for their freedom. . . . We act as we are bid by our revolutionary conscience, our Communist convictions.
>
> It is farthest from the Communists' minds to predict an "automatic collapse" of capitalism. It still has considerable reserves. Yet the developments of recent years forcefully confirm that capitalism is a society without a future. . . . the international situation of the Soviet Union has never been more solid . . . Socialism's positions have become stronger. Detente has become the leading trend. That is the main outcome of the party's international policy and Soviet people can be proud of it.

On the strength of these consistently voiced strategic concepts, Soviet leaders perceive their country is engaged in a long-drawn-out zero-sum game or contest with the United States, aiming at slow constriction of regions of the world where nations with capitalist economies can have access to, and mutual security arrangements with, one another. It is a strategy of conflict, to be kept below the intensity of total war but waged (in this era) to ease the United States out of the Eurasian continent as soon as feasible. The ultimate aim is strategic superiority, i.e., a position of power that cannot in the last analysis be challenged by any other likely combination of nations.

It has been asked, "What can you do with strategic superiority?" Soviet leaders think they know: intimidate and coerce other nations to organize totally controlled command economies that can be geared to support the economic strength of the USSR in the way that Poland, East Germany, and Czechoslovakia now do. The road there is to separate the United States from its transoceanic allies and bases and economic resources so that it will eventually become merely a hemispheric power—in a hemisphere that contains only a little over one quarter of the land surface of the globe. The nations of the Eurasian periphery and Africa would have nowhere to go but toward cooperation with the USSR. This Soviet approach to international affairs is a clear and coherent strategy, regardless of whether it can ever be carried out in reality. As a result the USSR must be granted high marks with respect to the effectiveness of its strategy for its national purposes.

The Strategic Concepts of Communist China (PRC)

The existence of the People's Republic of China (PRC) complicates every calculation in Moscow and Washington. In terms of the concrete elements of national power, the PRC is not near to being an equal of the United States or the Soviet Union. Nevertheless, the tradition of China as the Celestial Central Kingdom lingers on. Communist China considers itself the ultimate central kingdom of world Communist states, and as such, eventually the greatest power on earth. The Oriental time frame is long and Chinese patience and endurance are great. Still, within its limited capacities, Peking acts even now as the main strategic antagonist of the USSR and the United States. Communist China's global strategy must be understood if we are to assess perceptions of the world balance of power accurately.

As in the case of the USSR, there are serious doubts as to how and when Communist China will be able to reach the ambitious goals it has set for itself. Tactical caution and restraint are often dominant in Peking's policy, but the ultimate aim of the Chinese Communist Party is clear. Mao himself pronounced the word and it is taught throughout China as infallible wisdom—what is called "Mao Tse-tung thought." The Chinese claim that Mao made a crucial contribution to modern Communist doctrine and that the USSR under Khrushchev and Brezhnev is no longer a true Communist state but is instead a "social imperialist" society as bad as, or even worse than, the United States, the archetype of capitalist imperialism. This charge has made present-day China anathema to Soviet Communist Party leaders, who compare Mao to Stalin in his most savage days and countercharge that Mao's China does not properly belong to the Communist camp at all but instead has turned into a nationalist military dictatorship.

The crucial concepts of Mao Tse-tung thought on class conflict and war are similar to those of Lenin and Stalin, both of whom Mao retains in the Communist pantheon:[9]

> The enemy will not perish of himself. Neither the Chinese reactionaries nor the aggressive forces of U.S. imperialism in China will step down from the stage of history of their own accord. (1948)
>
> The seizure of power by armed force, the settlement of the issue by war, is the central task and the highest form of revolution. This Marxist-Leninist principle of revolution holds good universally, for China and for all other countries. (1938)

Mao's views on the United States prior to the diplomatic about-face which led him to accept detente and to welcome Nixon in Peking were extremely hostile:

> Riding rough-shod everywhere, U.S. imperialism has made itself the enemy of the people of the world and has increasingly isolated itself. . . . The raging tide of the people of the world against the U.S. aggressors is irresistible. (1964)
>
> If the U.S. monopoly capitalist groups persist in pushing their policies of aggression and war, the day is bound to come when they will be hanged by the people of the whole world. The same fate awaits the accomplices of the United States. (1958)

The Chinese were still busy painting over wall slogans about "U.S. aggressors and all their running dogs" when Nixon arrived in Peking in 1972.

Probably the most romantic and yet authentic explanation of the long-term strategy of Communist China since it has consolidated its power position was given by Lin Piao when he was defense minister and aspirant for the position of heir-apparent to Mao. In 1965 he made a policy statement called "Strategy and Tactics of a People's War," published in the Peking newspaper *Renmin Ribao* on September 3, 1965.[10] Some of the passages require a great deal of explication to be understood and, of course, relate very directly to the internal argument in China at that time about the proper reaction to U.S. intervention in the Vietnam War. Needless to say, the upshot of the policy debate was to support the Vietnamese but not to become directly involved in a conflict with the United States. After a long preamble Lin Piao took up the international significance of Mao's thinking:

> The Chinese revolution and the October Revolution have in common the following basic characteristics: Both were led by the working class with a Marxist-Leninist Party as its nucleus. . . . In both cases state power was seized through violent revolution and the dictatorship of the proletariat was established. . . . Both were component parts of the proletarian world revolution.
>
> It must be emphasized that Comrade Mao Tse-tung's theory of the establishment of rural revolutionary base areas and the encirclement of the cities from the countryside is of outstanding and universal practical importance for the present revolutionary struggles of all the oppressed nations and peoples, and particularly for the revolutionary struggles of the oppressed nations and peoples in Asia, Africa, and Latin America against imperialism and its lackeys.

Mao's disciple then laid out that extraordinary vision of Chinese leadership of the Third World against the industrial superpowers which seems to be the ultimate goal of the Mao generation of Chinese Communist leaders:

> Taking the entire globe, if North America and Western Europe can be called 'the cities of the world,' then Asia, Africa, and Latin America constitute 'the rural areas of the world.' Since World War II, the proletarian revolutionary movement has for various reasons

been temporarily held back in the North American and West Europe capitalist countries, while the people's revolutionary movement in Asia, Africa, and Latin America has been growing vigorously. In a sense the contemporary world revolution also presents a picture of the encirclement of cities by the rural areas. In the final analysis, the whole cause of world revolution hinges on the revolutionary struggles of the Asian, African, and Latin American peoples who make up the overwhelming majority of the world's population. The Socialist countries should regard it as their internationalist duty to support the people's revolutionary struggles in Asia, Africa, and Latin America.

History has proved and will go on proving that people's war is the most effective weapon against the U.S. imperialism and its lackeys. All revolutionary people will learn to wage people's war against U.S. imperialism and its lackeys. They will take up arms, learn to fight battles, and become skilled in waging people's war, though they have not done so before. U.S. imperialism, like a mad bull dashing from place to place, will finally be burned to ashes in the blazing fires of the people's wars it has provoked by its own actions.

This vision appears to explain the efforts which Peking has made to place itself at the head of the states representing the populous, poor, and colored nations of the world since the United States acquiesced in the entry of the People's Republic into the United Nations. Lin Piao of course perished during the course of a domestic power conflict in September 1971, but his fantasy of encircling the "cities of the world" lingers.

It is not that Peking expects these dreams to materialize immediately but that in the long run it wants to make the Chinese Communist Party the wave of the future, displacing present-day Soviet Communism as a model for revolution and gradually tightening the strategic encirclement of both the United States and the USSR. Perhaps Peking's strategic attitude toward the two superpowers is reflected in an old Chinese saying: "Sit on the mountain and watch the tigers fight each other."

Chinese strategy made one major change in the 1960s, as a result of the Sino-Soviet split. The bitter antagonism between the two ideological rivals is crucial in the power equation of the 1970s. It is not immutable although it stems from deep cultural and political antipathies.

Whether or not the rift will be papered over so that the two nations can cooperate in working against the interests of other states is one of the great imponderables of the post-Mao world. The bitterly competitive way in which Moscow and Peking approached the Vietnam War and yet gave Hanoi the military and economic support it needed, gives some disturbing evidence of the trend in the future. Nevertheless the continuing Sino-Soviet split divides much of Eurasia between these two hostile giants and the United States remains a lesser enemy of the PRC although still an enemy.

Since 1972 Communist China has attempted to stand between the two superpowers, playing them off against each other while trying to solve its own difficult problems of economic growth and of orderly political succession. Mao's death in 1976 has brought disorder and a sharp internal power struggle to mainland China. The regime under Mao's present successor, Hua Kuo-feng, continues to glorify Mao's thought and has not evoked a new international strategy.

If the power position of China were equivalent in economic strength and modern weapons-technology with its self-esteem and ambition, Peking would have greater effect with this heavy class-war revolutionary rhetoric. Since the power base is weak and Communist China will do well to feed its burgeoning population during the next 10 or 20 years, China must be perceived as having a clear national strategy but one that presently functions more in the realm of propaganda than of action outside the regional Asian context. Moreover, uncertainty about the ultimate victors in the succession struggles that burst out with the arrest of Mao's widow, Chiang Ching, and her supporters among the more visionary Maoist revolutionary ideologues, leaves quasi-independent military leaders and practical managerial bureaucrats to work out a political *modus vivendi*. Strategy could move in almost any direction. At present, then, China has the strategic concepts and political ambition of a great global power, but it does not yet have stable national strategy or a unified national will to support its long-range revolutionary goals.

Strategic Thinking in the United States

Strategy in any nation under a system of representative government and multiparty elections is bound to be more diffuse than it is in a totalitarian dictatorship where a comparatively small number of leaders are able to make secret and authoritative decisions. The strategy of the United States must be approached through its historical conduct of international affairs much more than in its pronouncements of political purpose, which are usually designed to win the widest possible popular support rather than to delineate future national action. Moreover, much of U.S. policy is reactive, designed in response to situations created by other nations. Therefore over the past 30 years U.S. strategy has been defined through a pattern of actions and goals worked out within the framework of relations with the USSR, the only power competing with the United States on a more or less equal basis.

The United States relied during most of its history on a policy of avoiding entangling international commitments, counting on the vigor of the nineteenth-century British Empire to protect the western hemisphere from hostile intrusion. Despite a brief emergence into a wider world in World War I, the United States still clung to hemispheric isolation and neutrality with regard to international conflicts through the 1930s. All of this ended abruptly in 1941 when Pearl Harbor vividly confirmed the argument of the interventionists of the period that the United States could not stay out of world conflicts but had instead an obligation to protect the interests of U.S. citizens through positive action to ameliorate the international climate in which we have to live.

Preserving "democracy" is somewhat too vague to be helpful in defining goals, although it suggests a policy of attempting to protect the U.S. system of representative government, free elections, constitutional checks and balances, and guarantees of individual and minority rights in a pluralistic society. Yet, in the perception of most Americans, our foreign policy ought to preserve the U.S. open society and the prosperity based on free-enterprise economics. This aim has been the bedrock of U.S. strategy. President Kennedy put it succinctly when he said repeatedly in the last year of his life that the United States was striving for a world safe for diversity as distinct from totalitarianism. If there is a moral element in U.S. foreign policy, it is a determined preference for the pluralistic society and an affirmation of the right of individuals in all parts of the world to determine the kind of society they want. This political philosophy implies resistance to the spread of totalitarianism, whether by direct or by indirect aggression.

Evolution of U.S. Strategic Concepts in the "American Age"

U.S. national strategy since 1945 has tended to be dominated by U.S. concern about the hostile intentions of the USSR. There has, however, also been a strong positive strand of strategic thinking about the importance of our allies and of worldwide economic stability. The 30 years after the end of World War II were marked by almost incidental accretions of U.S. influence in regions of the world which wanted assistance because the local leaders feared military domination or internal political subversion sponsored by the USSR or, later, by Communist China. The United States has exhibited little appetite for seizing and holding real imperial power.

Gradually, in 1947 and later, U.S. leaders, rightly or wrongly, thought that the great danger of this period lay in the establishment of a permanent controlling influence in many foreign countries by Soviet-dominated Communist regimes. East Europe soon became a belt of nations ruled by one-party Communist dictatorships committed to cooperation with the policies of the Soviet Union. The economically devastated nations of West Europe were not secure against the same political evolution.

In the beginning, most U.S. citizens did not feel any serious fear of war, but they did worry that the political and economic conditions in West Europe would create a power vacuum tempting to the Soviet Union under Stalin. Increasingly the USSR came to be viewed as a threat to the security of West Europe because of active Soviet support of Communist Parties in East Europe.

At the time the United States felt fairly confident of its own position in the world. After all, the total economic activity in the United States (GNP) was 480 billion U.S. dollars (rounded, in 1973 dollars). In the same terms, the Soviet Union's GNP was approximately 150 billion (1973) U.S. dollars. This comfortable margin of superiority of more than three to one in gross measurement of economic strength supplied the United States with a surplus which enabled it to raise the standard of living of its own people rapidly—something the Soviet Union was quite unable to do—and at the same time to disperse its money in vast amounts to restore and stimulate economic production in West Europe and elsewhere. Here was a situation of strategic superiority based on economic strength which clearly could be used, and was used, to exercise U.S. influence in Europe in ways designed to prevent major aggrandizement by a large and increasingly hostile power, the USSR. At the same time, the humane instincts of the U.S. people were satisfied with respect to restoring civilized life in an area of the world from whose cultures most citizens of the United States had come.

The "Containment" Strategy

What was to become the classic text of U.S. strategic policy for many years was published in the July 1947 issue of *Foreign Affairs* in an article by "Mr. X," who was George Kennan, then State Department policy planner for Secretary of State George C. Marshall. While it is very simply stated, most of the Kennan essay still provides a coherent rationale for U.S. international behavior from that time into the late 1960s.

The "Mr. X" article recommended adoption of a U.S. "policy of firm containment, designed to confront the Russians with unalterable counter-force at every point where they show signs of encroaching upon the interests of a peaceful and stable world."

Most people in the United States who had lived through the 1930s and 1940s thought they had learned the need for early resistance to a dangerous aggressor because it had cost the world so much to let Manchuria be occupied by Japan, Ethiopia by Italy, and Austria and Czechoslovakia by Germany, prior to World War II. Allowing small nations to be toppled one by one by forces external to the nation had only made the ultimate showdown harder. For a long time, until the fall of South Vietnam, this conviction played an integral part in U.S. strategy.

Vital to this containment policy was the strengthening of the free-world economy and the development of a free-world alliance. The economic spread of Soviet influence could best be stopped in Europe by the economic rebuilding of Germany, Italy, France, and other nations close to the USSR. It was perceived that West Europe had to be helped to become socially stable in order to resist internal subversion by the Communist Party or other pro-Soviet organizations. Hence the Marshall Plan. In the military sphere, a parallel move set up the North

U.S.-USSR Relations Since World War II

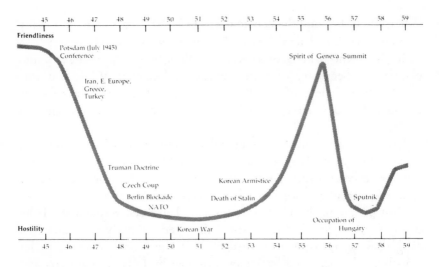

Atlantic Treaty Organization to stiffen military defense of the area and relieve fears that the massive conventional Soviet armies in East Germany might suddenly roll over West Europe.

Containment in this era seemed to require a global trading network that strengthened every nation not already under a Communist regime, particularly all of those in the U.S. alliance system. U.S. aid strengthened and protected vast areas sheltering under the umbrella of U.S.

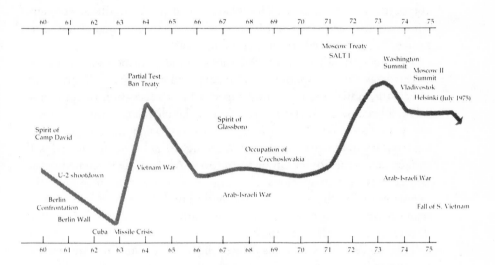

commitments. It is hard to say whether fear of the USSR and mainland China held this loose association of nations together or whether the positive economic benefits of trade and aid were responsible. Almost certainly both aspects contributed to the cohesion of the U.S. alliance system. Containment and alliance building were two sides of the same coin of U.S. strategy in this era.

U.S.-Soviet Diplomatic Atmospherics

Pursuit of the combined alliance containment strategy brought relative security and prosperity to the United States for many years. For one thing, it made strong U.S. allies out of its World War II enemies, Germany and Japan. Throughout this period, however, attention focused on the crucial bilateral U.S.-Soviet relationship, and the theatrics of this great power rivalry tended to obscure the real strategic competition, as well as the vital character of the U.S. alliance system. These atmospherics, which Moscow is able to turn on and off on short notice, are illustrated in the preceding chart.

The Cuba missile crisis of 1962 shocked and disturbed people almost as much as the occupation of Hungary and the Korean War. In its aftermath, however, there developed a brief relaxation of tension—relaxed because of Soviet recognition of the clear-cut strategic superiority of the United States and the demonstration that, in a serious confrontation, the government in Washington had the courage and skill to face down the Soviet Union with force. At the time it seemed in the United States a marvelous clearing of the air, and provided the opportunity for the greatest diplomatic breakthrough in U.S.-Soviet relations in the postwar era, the negotiation of the Partial Test-Ban Treaty of 1963 with the USSR.

This success in Cuba may later have given an impetus to the overcommitment of U.S. resources and the misguided policy of deliberately slow escalation of fighting in Vietnam. U.S. and Soviet policymakers were soon caught up in the struggle for control of the Indochina peninsula. In 1965 and 1966, both great powers were supporting opponents in what looked like another "proxy war" of the Korean type but was in fact complicated by the crosscurrents of Indochinese politics. It ended up with massive U.S. forces fighting with indifferent success an enormous guerrilla army directed from Hanoi and supported economically and logistically by both China and the USSR.

The hostility generated by the Vietnam situation was aggravated in some ways by the Arab-Israeli War of 1967. An attempt to reestablish an atmosphere of friendliness by the meeting of President Johnson and Prime Minister Kosygin gave only a brief respite—a shallow, insubstantial "Spirit of Glassboro"—punctuating the atmospheric trend.

Hostility soon reached another high point as a result of the Soviet decision to occupy Czechoslovakia in 1968 and prevent the "Prague Spring," with its enthusiasm for bringing forward the "human face" of Communism, from getting out of hand and compromising Soviet control in the most progressive and sophisticated of the East European nations.

Soviet strategic policy was thenceforth crystal clear, in accordance with the "Brezhnev doctrine" that the USSR would send military forces to police any country ruled by a Communist Party if Moscow foresaw a danger of the "restoration of the capitalist order." Brezhnev declared, according to an article in *Pravda* in September of 1968, that a threat to "the cause of socialism" in any country was a "threat to the security of the socialist (i.e., Communist) community as a whole" and therefore became "no longer a problem for the people of that country but also a common problem, a concern for all socialist states." In other words, the USSR gave what seemed to be an iron-clad guarantee that there was no going back when any country adopted a Soviet-oriented Communist form of government.

The Age of Detente, 1969-1975

Strangely, the occupation of Czechoslovakia and the Brezhnev security guarantee of the "socialist community" did not seem to generate the same indignation as the occupation of Hungary had more than a decade earlier, and, beginning in 1969, hostility slowly began to diminish in the wake of a determined Soviet campaign emphasizing peaceful coexistence and the relaxation of international tension—which gradually came to be called by the more ambiguous term detente. The waning of public support in the United States for the Vietnam War paralleled and partially caused U.S. adoption of detente as its foreign policy.

The latest phase of U.S.-Soviet relations has brought the diplomatic atmosphere in which these relations are conducted closer to the "Spirit of Geneva" than at any other time in the postwar period. This change was accomplished principally through the deliberate policy of the Nixon administration of endorsing the Soviet concept of peaceful coexistence. The strong U.S. expression of interest in restricting the further growth of costly strategic weapons systems, very congenial to Moscow, where top political and military leaders envy and fear U.S. weapons technology, reinforced the new U.S. foreign policy trend.

The comparative harmony of 1972 and 1973 saw the Moscow Treaty and Moscow Summit Meeting, the conclusion of SALT I, and the Washington Summit in the summer of 1973. This harmony was widely acclaimed in the United States as leading to a "generation of peace" and closing out the Cold War forever.

The USSR, discovering that the people of the United States enjoyed the word detente very much, whatever it might mean, did everything possible to suggest to the outside world—as distinct from its own officials—that a new era was at hand quite different from the period of twenty-odd years when containment was the keynote of U.S. policy. The momentum toward improved relations was hard to maintain, however, because of very real continuing conflicts of interest between the USSR and the United States.

The most significant clash of recent years came in the Mideast when the Arab-Israeli War broke out in October 1973, with an attack by Egypt and Syria. Massive amounts of modern Soviet weapons were employed by the two Arab states and it became necessary for the United States to resupply Israel on a crash basis to insure its survival.

Nevertheless, the governments in both Moscow and Washington forged ahead in an effort to maintain that detente was a unique and valuable accomplishment of Nixon-Kissinger/Brezhnev collaboration and that it would persist in bringing the United States and the USSR closer together. In fact, it is hard to plot a curve of relationships between the USSR and the United States without turning it away from cooperation in the fall of 1973, on through 1974, and into 1975. Not the least of the difficulties in the way of amicable U.S.-Soviet relations was the preoccupation of the Nixon administration with Watergate.

A somewhat ambivalent state of affairs, with protestations of good intentions coming from both capitals but with very little solid progress being made, set in during the summer of 1974 when the highly advertised Moscow II Summit Meeting and SALT II deliberations produced almost no results whatever. Perhaps a modest gain was registered as a result of an agreement on equivalence of numbers of strategic weapons (at very high levels) at President Ford's meeting with Brezhnev in Vladivostok, but this still has to be translated into a treaty.

At this stage, it is impossible to tell whether the determination of the two governments to maintain the atmosphere of comparative cordiality will be able to dominate events despite crucial strategic conflicts of interest. The language of the odd assortment of agreements and undertakings on European security and economic cooperation signed in Helsinki at the end of July 1975 was interpreted differently in Moscow and Washington, particularly with respect to human rights. The USSR clamped tighter controls on its dissident citizens and U.S. criticisms grew louder.

The line of reasoning which holds out hope that continued discussion with the USSR will bring about reorientation of Soviet thinking away from conflict and toward cooperation is an entirely legitimate hope. It is not a certainty. It is not a substitute for a foreign policy. It became less promising as tension in the Mideast continued, as a squabble over the right of Soviet citizens to emigrate prevented trade expansion between the USSR and the United States, and as the Vietnam peace treaty collapsed in a total victory for Hanoi in the spring of 1975.

After the USSR in the fall of 1975 provided generous arms support to the guerrilla faction friendly to it in Angola and encouraged Cuba to send its own armed forces to put this faction in command as the new government of Angola, the architecture of detente—oversold to the U.S. public and to U.S. allies—came under increasing criticism. It was suggested in Washington that for the United States detente is a policy of placating enemies by alienating allies.

The Ford administration undertook a partial return to some of the strategic concepts of earlier years, stressing U.S. alliances and refusing to cut defense expenditures on the basis of hopes about the fruits of detente. The climate of detente lingered on, however, and Kissinger defended its benefits, no matter how limited, by saying there is no alternative except nuclear war. Of course there is an alternative, and that is the kind of continuous political and economic conflict of lower intensity visualized by the USSR as the essence of peaceful coexistence. In view of these ambiguities as to priorities and purposes in dealing with the USSR, as distinct from strengthening U.S. alliances, it is not surprising that there has been some confusion of Congress, the people, and opinion-makers about the coherence of U.S. strategy. Strategically, the United States appeared to be drifting as it moved from its bicentennial year into 1977.

Since grand diplomacy dropped into a relatively sterile mode there has been little clarification of national strategy. The Watergate political tragedy taught the U.S. public to be suspicious of authoritative leadership; so that there now exists no consensus as to what the goals of U.S. relations with the USSR and China, or of U.S. alliance commitments, should be. It has become unclear in the perceptions of Americans as well as those of many nations' leaders exactly what the United States stands for and would fight for. Hence its rating is still low for the subjective factors of strategy and will as elements of national power.

The celebration of the two centuries of independent U.S. history throughout 1976 seemed to give a lift to American spirits. The scars of Vietnam and Watergate began to fade. The Carter administration came into office in 1977 on a tide of criticism of detente-justified concessions to the USSR, a demand for greater moral dedication to human rights as the basis of national policy, and some blooming of hope for a recovery of U.S. morale and leadership in world affairs. The basic power position of the United States remains strong in 1977. With key alliances in other regions and with the survival of present international trade patterns, the United States with its existing alliance system is superior in potential power to any likely adversary or combination of adversaries.

If U.S. political leaders move consistently in 1977 in a clear national strategic direction, the people of the United States would like to know once again for sure who our enemies are, what dangers to the United States they represent, or what is strategically important abroad. More on the basis of hope than achievement, the United States is entering its third century with a feeling of more unified national will than existed two years ago. If the national strategy comes into clearer focus, the perceptions of the United States as an international power will again reach the heights commensurate with the concrete elements of its strength.

The Rest of the World

It is a reflection of the way global power is perceived in this era that we can turn from the three nations with pretensions to a broad, world-encompassing strategy to observe that the other 155 independent nations and more than two and one-half billion people are pursuing regional strategies and trying to manipulate to advantage one way or another relationships with the USSR, the United States, and China (PRC). This psychological-political phenomenon complicates the life of policymakers in Moscow, Washington, and Peking and makes international forces extremely fluid. The balance of power is changing from a period of U.S.

dominance and is unstable. A few sudden key shifts could cause a movement of politectonic power clusters from one zone of influence to another.

In North America the two large neighbors of the United States have enjoyed reasonably close relations with Washington, but this is less true now than in the day of clearer articulation of U.S. strategy. Both Canada and Mexico at present strongly stress independence from the United States despite geographically-determined economic and military interdependence. This strategic inconsistency requires a reduction in the coefficient for this factor. Anti-Yankee sentiment is not a substitute for a coherent strategy for these two important U.S. neighbors. Thus the increment to power of North America is not as great as what is implied by the size and economic strength of the two nations. Their military power is also limited because they do not feel the need to invest large percentages of GNP in defense while they remain under the U.S. military deterrent shield and yet identify imperfectly with U.S. strategy.

In East Europe, Poland and East Germany are subject to the political discipline of police states occupied by massive Soviet armies. Because they are required to follow Soviet strategy without question and because public consent does not play a large part in decision-making, the power of these states is enhanced by a comparatively high coefficient for strategy. The national will is reduced, however, because the people in countries that are virtually occupied states most often lend fairly lethargic support to Soviet goals and on occasion are actively restless and resistant to Soviet policies.

West Europe is not a unity in any true strategic sense, although each nation in NATO gains some sense of coherent national strategy as a result of NATO collaboration and the strategic leadership of the United States. The national will in these countries varies according to the domestic political situation. The United Kingdom articulates Atlantic goals effectively but is much reduced from its former levels of political and economic drive. Germany, the most closely identified with European U.S.-NATO strategy and the most politically disciplined, receives high marks for its sense of national purpose. Both Spain and Yugoslavia are unique, with reasonably clear strategies (to stay close to the United States and West Europe in the case of the former and to stay nonaligned and independent in the case of the latter). In both of these nations, the domestic political situation is sufficiently unsettled to raise grave doubts about a future political unity.

In the remaining rimlands of Eurasia, the key countries from Egypt and Turkey around to Japan are all uncertain about their strategic future and about the degree of political consensus in their conduct of foreign affairs. Their aims are for the most part regional or local or almost tribal.

Finally, the outer circle of states geographically more remote from the great-power conflicts is taking advantage of this distance to pursue largely regional policies. These states differ in their clarity of strategic purpose and internal political structure. Brazil, Nigeria, and Australia are dynamic economically and psychologically, but are largely regional and somewhat parochial in their strategic and political ambitions in this decade. South Africa has such serious domestic, social, and political problems that it is on the defensive internationally.

Strategy and Will: Final Ratings

Judgments about this final factor in the formula we have been using are bound to be mainly qualitative, rather than precise and quantitative; it would be unproductive to describe and defend in detail the coefficients assigned.[11]

Prudence suggests that no attempt be made to rate most of the less powerful nations of the world for national strategy and national will. A few exceptions, however, are rather compelling. Some smaller powers with strong governments, whether democratic or totalitarian, and clear national goals, must be rated and ranked anew. Some, like Rumania, Cuba, Israel, Singapore, and New Zealand, take on a special signifi- cance because of their strategic locations linking them with larger countries. For example, Rumania is on the edge of the Soviet-dominated zone maneuvering for its independence; Cuba is in the U.S. zone of influence but presently committed to the USSR; Israel is virtually a U.S. outpost in a dangerous sea of Mideast states. Singapore is a key commercial entrepot and—with Indonesia—a co-custodian of the Malacca Straits. New Zealand is culturally and strategically tied to Australia and, to some extent, to the United States.

On this basis 56 nations in all are ranked for perceived powers in the following table.

Final Assessment

Zone	Country	Concrete Elements of Perceived Power	National Strategy	National Will	Total Coefficient	Total	Perceived Power Weights: Zonal Total
I	United States	468	0.4	0.5	0.9	421	523
	Canada	97	0.2	0.4	0.6	58	
	Mexico	74	0.2	0.4	0.6	44	
II	USSR	402	0.8	0.5	1.3	523	618
	Poland	48	0.5	0.2	0.7	34	
	Mongolia	30	0.3	0.1	0.4	12	
	Rumania	24	0.5	0.5	1.0	24	
	East Germany (GDR)	22	0.8	0.2	1.0	22	
	Cuba	2	0.7	0.6	1.3	3	
III	PRC	171	0.5	0.2	0.7	120	209
	Vietnam	48	0.8	0.4	1.2	58	
	North Korea	22	0.8	0.6	1.4	31	
IV	West Germany (FRG)	112	0.7	0.8	1.5	168	558
	France	112	0.4	0.5	0.9	101	
	United Kingdom	99	0.6	0.4	1.0	99	
	Italy	71	0.5	0.3	0.8	57	
	Spain	59	0.5	0.4	0.9	53	
	Yugoslavia	36	0.5	0.2	0.7	25	
	Sweden	29	0.5	0.7	1.2	35	
	Norway	20	0.5	0.5	1.0	25	
V	Iran	80	0.9	0.7	1.6	128	483
	Egypt	65	0.5	0.6	1.1	72	
	Turkey	65	0.2	0.4	0.6	39	
	Saudi Arabia	43	0.7	0.7	1.4	60	
	Algeria	41	0.5	0.5	1.0	41	
	Sudan	40	0.2	0.3	0.5	20	
	Libya	33	0.5	0.6	1.1	36	
	Morocco	30	0.5	0.5	1.0	30	
	Iraq	25	0.3	0.5	0.8	20	
	Israel	22	0.9	0.8	1.7	37	

Zone	Country	Concrete Elements of Perceived Power	National Strategy	National Will	Total Coefficient	Total	Perceived Power Weights: Zonal Total
VI	India	97	0.3	0.3	0.6	58	164
	Pakistan	62	0.5	0.5	1.0	62	
	Bangladesh	40	0.3	0.2	0.5	20	
	Afghanistan	30	0.5	0.3	0.8	24	
VII	Indonesia	85	0.5	0.5	1.0	85	172
	Singapore	1	0.5	0.5	1.0	1	
	Burma	50	0.2	0.1	0.3	15	
	Thailand	47	0.5	0.3	0.8	38	
	Philippines	41	0.5	0.3	0.8	33	
VIII	Japan	111	0.5	0.8	1.3	144	234
	South Korea	38	0.7	0.7	1.4	53	
	China/Taiwan	23	0.7	0.9	1.6	37	
IX	Brazil	94	0.5	0.8	1.3	122	282
	Argentina	71	0.3	0.2	0.5	36	
	Colombia	41	0.5	0.5	1.0	41	
	Peru	31	0.5	0.5	1.0	31	
	Venezuela	26	0.5	0.5	1.0	26	
	Chile	22	0.5	0.7	1.2	26	
X	Nigeria	65	0.4	0.4	0.8	52	233
	South Africa	60	0.6	0.4	1.0	60	
	Zaire	55	0.5	0.5	1.0	55	
	Ethiopia	45	0.1	0.2	0.3	14	
	Tanzania	30	0.5	0.5	1.0	30	
	Zambia	22	0.5	0.5	1.0	22	
XI	Australia	60	0.4	0.7	1.1	66	77
	New Zealand	11	0.5	0.5	1.0	11	

TOTAL FOR ALL ZONES (56 nations)   3,553

The striking fact that emerges from this table and from the entire method of analysis followed in this book is that national purpose and national will make a critical difference in the relative power of nations. A totalitarian system has many shortcomings and its suppression of individual freedom and initiative cripples the development of a high level of achievement within a society. Nevertheless, the fact that the USSR has a coherent strategy and a tightly controlled population multiplies the brute power it projects into the international arena. The rating of 523 derives from the efficiency of Soviet decision-making and the discipline enforced on the Soviet people; it is diminished by the dulled responsivity of a population inured to dictatorship and by the divisive element of tension between Slav and non-Slav peoples.[12]

The Chinese system has some of the same advantages, but it lacks a truly coherent national policy at this juncture, despite its ambition, because Chinese leaders are jockeying for position in the struggle for power after Mao's death. The nation is not yet unified in pursuit of its long-range strategy and hence its coefficient for national will is low.

Clarity of national purpose and coherence of disciplined political will also show up in the ratings of countries like West Germany, Iran, China/Taiwan, and Israel. Most of the coefficients for the nations rated can be derived fairly readily from their current history.

For the United States a below-normal coefficient for strategy and will must be assigned as of mid-1977, but one that is higher than in mid-1975. The political malaise left as a legacy of Watergate, Vietnam, and the illusions of easily attained mutually beneficial detente has yet to be dispelled. The debilitation of the National Security Council decision-making system under Nixon and the breakdown of congressional-presidential cooperation in strategic and international policy formulation leave a legacy of uncertainty and still grave functional handicaps;[13] fortunately, however, President Ford's and President Carter's preferences for more open decision-making and caution, candor, simplicity, and loyalty to alliances have started to move the United States in the right direction.

The best thing that can be said today is that U.S. political moods are volatile and its people are resilient. There is a bubbling up of the American spirit; the pendulum is beginning to swing back from pessimism toward increased confidence. The United States is capable of formulating anew a reasonable strategic policy and building a consensus in support of it. If this occurs, U.S. power will again rise to high levels.

National purpose and national will are the most critical factors in determining power. The tremendous power potential of a country like the United States can be fully achieved only when its political leadership is unified and crystal clear in explaining national security strategy and foreign policy. With a new White House team of the same political party as the majority of the Congress, all of this can happen during the course of 1977. In these circumstances, as the highpoints of World War II and the late 1950s-early 1960s show, an open society with the support of the governed becomes virtually invincible in international affairs.

CHAPTER EIGHT

Shaping a New Foreign Policy for Americans

F rom the foregoing analysis it is plain that there is some truth in the common perception that the United States has lost momentum and impact in recent international affairs. In great part this perception stems from the fact that defeat in Vietnam and failure to prevent Soviet-Cuban establishment of paramount influence in Angola spelled the end of the U.S. strategy of general containment. Worse, the United States drifted away from its old strategy without formulating any other purpose around which the nation's energies can be mobilized. Americans are muddled in their thinking about the outside world and the national will is as a consequence unfocused and flabby. Thus the United States projects an image of weakness despite its immense strength. What is needed is straightforward, candid leadership that can think out and pursue at home and abroad a coherent course for the United States to steer in its international relations.

It is hard to believe that the sense of self-preservation and self-interest of the people of the United States has been permanently enfeebled by the Vietnam defeat and Watergate's discrediting of national government. It ought to become clearer and clearer that stopping the drift of the last few years in U.S. foreign policy is essential if politectonic shifts are not to cause whole regions to slide away from the present alliance structure that makes U.S. security and economic prosperity possible.

The first step is to clarify the true strategic challenge of our time. The danger is not that in the foreseeable future the USSR will rain nuclear bombs on American cities nor that Soviet armies will roll to the Rhine. The United States and its closest allies are still too strong in strategic, conventional, and tactical nuclear forces to make outright military attacks profitable for the USSR. The Soviet leaders do not want to destroy the industry and technology of West Europe; they want to dominate the area and exploit it economically. They do not want to fight a war with the United States; they want to separate the United States from its allies.

The PRC is, of course, comparatively much weaker and less tempted to try a military path in moving toward Chinese Communist goals at this point in history. The real threat is simply that neither the USSR nor the PRC is content to let the balance of power remain in its present state of rough equilibrium between totalitarian states and the pluralist societies associated with the United States. They are dedicated to making what the Soviet leaders call an irreversible gain in the correlation of forces by breaking American political and economic links with as many as possible of the nations that now look to the United States to protect their security.

Moscow and Peking differ over the way in which pluralist societies will come to their final destruction but both are committed to a grand strategy of creating situations hostile to the projection of American influence across the seas and ultimately hostile to the very survival of the social and political organization that exists in the United States. It has been fashionable for some years for Americans to gloss over this fundamental antagonism emanating from Communist capitals. A realistic foreign policy must be based on recognition that the rulers of the USSR and the PRC are thinking in adversary terms in every kind of interaction with the United States. No amount of charm and diplomacy, nor any number of generous concessions, will change this Soviet viewpoint in the next decade or two.

The so-called American Age of the post-World War II era may have had its shortcomings on the side of unrealistic idealism. Nevertheless, the post-World War II containment policy provided a grand strategy centered in defending a nontotalitarian was of life that was understandable and congenial to most Americans. The concept of U.S. responsibility for the security and freedom of every single part of the world is now unviable. Boundaries of spheres of influence have been broken down by the Cubans, the Vietnamese, and the Angolans. Something is urgently needed to serve the same national purpose for the United States in the 1970s.

An Oceans Alliance

From the outset I have made it clear in this book that my own recommended remedy is what I call a new Athenian League, a voluntary association of selected nations maintaining the security of a transoceanic alliance system built around the strength and leadership of the United States.[1] My preferred name for it is an Oceans Alliance, broader than the Atlantic Alliance and broader even than the Trilateral Alliance, which embraces Japan as well as West Europe but is not truly global.

Members of an Oceans Alliance would have a mutual obligation to one another to prevent the domination of their own territory by the totalitarian states of Zones II and III. Success in this obligation would in fact protect all of the nations of consequence in the Eurasian rimlands, Zones IV through VII. To some extent this strategy is a variation on the theme of containment, but it is a new, realistic strategy of selective containment. To put it positively rather than negatively, U.S. grand strategy, as distinct from military strategy, should be formulated and made public in terms along the lines suggested in Chapter One:

> The United States should protect the security of its people and society by maintaining an alliance system of nations with nontotalitarian societies which will prevent a totalitarian nation or combination of such nations from establishing political or military control over all of central Eurasia (the region now controlled by the USSR) *plus* any substantial parts of the Eurasian peripheral rimlands.

The hallmark of an Oceans Alliance would be a firm strategic commitment by the United States to defend the specific major nations of each politectonic zone that join in a voluntary security association with one another and with the United States.

These selective commitments would not necessarily be exclusive. The United States should make it clear that it is not flatly rejecting responsibility for the security of other regions. Some degree of strategic uncertainty as to the exact extent of the U.S. willingness to defend lesser nations is a positive plus in that it is a deterrent factor in the minds of war planners in other capitals. They should not be able to be certain, as the Soviet and North Korean leaders thought they were in South Korea in 1950, that a country is outside the sphere of U.S. protection.

What an Oceans Alliance would do is stake out key areas where U.S. interests are unmistakenly paramount. The United States should build its alliance from the center out, starting with a strong strategic deterrent and a strong military, i.e., war-fighting, capability. The grand strategy of the Oceans Alliance would then call for reaching out first in the North American Zone to improve our political, economic, and military relations with our neighbors to the north and south; and thence across the oceans to the members of the core group of allies on the Eurasian periphery, and finally to those other nations in each politectonic zone willing to share the burdens of becoming members of the new Oceans Alliance.

It follows, of course, that if the United States reaffirms its commitments to allies in keeping with this grand strategy, it must in its supporting military policy steadfastly maintain three basic programs. The United States must have in readiness and, even more important, have downstream in research and development, a series of advanced weapons systems constituting an (a) invulnerable deterrent against general strategic attack by any other nation; (b) sufficient strategic attack capability to project an image of parity in general strategic terms with any other nation, and (c) conventional or general purpose military forces in being that are truly "second to none" in terms of ability to reach out across the seas and protect the nations of the world that are part of the Oceans Alliance. The object of all aspects of this military policy is to prevent even the most militant-minded leaders in other nations from feeling that either a nuclear war or a conventional one might truly be won through temporary achievement of an overwhelming superiority in military weapons that would politically immobilize and paralyze U.S. resistance. In the present configuration of world power, the United States can carry out such a military policy with the annual expenditure of about 6 percent of its GNP, a bargain price for liberty and security.

One firm strategic benefit emerging from following an Oceans Alliance policy would be that around the globe and even inside the Soviet Union and the People's Republic of China many individuals will yearn for the human rights and minority privileges that they do not now enjoy. If the United States affirms these concepts as central to its grand strategy, it would tend to pull its own allies in the right political direction and at the same time make the citizenry and the bureaucracies of the totalitarian states and their subordinated nations, like Poland and Czechoslovakia, realize that there is another and better way of life less backward than the command economy and politics of the USSR. Insofar as the United States takes the offensive strategically beyond the confines of its Oceans Alliance, it should be only in this political sense and in the economic sense of asserting the creativeness and material benefits of a comparatively free and independent form of society. This grand strategy is not a war hawk policy; it is a way of keeping the peace through political, economic, and military strength adequate to maintain a balance in world power.

Core Allies

On the foundation of these principles the United States should focus its diplomacy on building an effective alliance, with adequate strength to counterbalance threats from Zone II or Zone III regimes. This is not too difficult a task, since these zones contain only a little over 800 perceived power weights of a world total of just over 3,500, according to my calculus. The United States cannot do it alone, nor can North America. The United States can, however, construct an alliance system that includes the leading nations able and willing to oppose Soviet and Chinese efforts to expand their spheres of influence. Such an alliance, to feel secure in an essentially defensive posture, ought to dispose of perceived power approximately twice as great as either the USSR in its whole Eurasian sphere of influence or the PRC in the Asian-Pacific region. With this structural concept in mind, anyone can select the number of key allies needed to cooperate with the United States in preserving a world safe for diversity and pluralist societies.

The first choices for membership in the core group of a new Oceans Alliance are bound to consist of the major states with similar political and social processes, as well as shared goals and views about international dangers: the United States, Canada, West Germany (FRG), France, the United Kingdom, Italy, Israel, Japan, China/Taiwan, and Australia.[2] These ten nations collectively possess one-third of the perceived power of the entire 56 nations we have singled out (Chapter Seven, pages 173-174) as being of highest international importance. This group of ten tends to set the strategic pattern in the four politectonic Zones I,

IV, VIII, and XI, which contains almost 900 million people, 14 million square miles of territory, and most of the world's advanced technology.

Substantial ethnic groups in the United States have emigrated from all of the countries selected above, bringing their cultural contributions to U.S. society. All have parliaments, relatively open electoral processes, and economic systems based on comparatively free international trade. It is easy to quibble about the effectiveness of national democratic procedures, including those in the United States, but these countries represent basically open societies operating under rules of law, with varying degrees of protection for civil rights, and with the consent of the governed.

The English-speaking nations have a long history of special bonds with one another and with the United States. Israel is a unique case, a country created by the United Nations and sustained by support from the United States and West Europe for a quarter-century of turbulent existence. Its close cultural and religious ties with Jewish communities in the United States are comparable to the ties of U.S. citizens of Chinese, Japanese, German, and Italian descent, and all the rest, with their ethnic homelands. Canada and Mexico are so close and so inextricably linked economically with the United States that they must be included.

Since World War II, Japan and China/Taiwan have closely associated themselves with the United States, the most economically and politically advanced nations in East Asia of all those to do so. They are almost totally dependent on U.S. treaties to guarantee their security against domination or conquest by mainland China. The government of the Republic of China in Taipei claims it is *de jure* the government of all China, but it is as the *de facto* government of the island of Taiwan and of the Pescadores that it is protected by its mutual defense treaty with the United States. The constitutionally proclaimed goal of this Chinese society, as distinct from the one on the mainland, is democratic government whenever the state of war is ended and political and economic conditions permit. Its island position, its modern export-oriented economy, and its substantial political progress toward democratic government in Taiwan in the face of still serious military threats from Peking, qualify it along with Japan as an Asian strong point in an Oceans Alliance.

Japan represents the only large population unit in Northeast Asia and is the leading proponent of modern economic technology based on world trade. The inclusion of these Northeast Asian states in the core group extends its reach from Asia and the Pacific across North America to connect with the leading nations of West Europe.

These ten nations can accomplish prodigies by working closely together. In terms of global strategy and geography, however, there is a dangerous gap on the southern periphery of Eurasia between Northeast Asia and West Europe—a gap that has to be filled by leading nations interested in maintaining the independence and freedom of their own regions from Soviet and Chinese domination. An Oceans Alliance must be sure its members are able to move and trade along routes running around the world through the Pacific, Indian, and Atlantic Oceans. These ten core group allies collectively muster almost twice the perceived strength of the Soviet sphere of influence (Zone II) as measured in this calculus (Chapter Seven, page 173), and well over five times the perceived strength of Communist Asia. In fact, the core allies dispose of more perceived power than exists among the leading nations of both Zone II and Zone III combined, but not by the comfortable two-to-one margin necessary to guarantee the security of a voluntary defensive alliance against powerful armed totalitarian states.

Consequently, beyond the ten already mentioned, equally close alliances should be built up with a number of other friendly nations, some of whom may have political traditions or social structures somewhat different from those of the United States. The Oceans Alliance ought to include at least one strong point in every politectonic zone in the Eurasian rimlands and the outer crescent of the southern hemisphere.

There is a great difference between an authoritarian political regime with a regard for the welfare of its citizens, and a rigidly totalitarian state determined to control the minds and actions of every person within its borders. The United States should welcome into the Oceans Alliance nations which at present have compelling reasons to follow political processes that do not fully qualify them as democratic, providing they have enough political support to govern in their own countries and do not emulate Soviet or Chinese models of totalitarianism. Iran and Brazil come to mind as nationalist authoritarian regimes with substantial consent of their governed. If such nations have significant elements of power, appear to have the general support of their people, and look to trade and to political contacts with the United States and its allies for future security and economic prosperity, they ought to be eligible to belong in the Oceans Alliance.

Nations that are suitable candidates, in addition to those already mentioned, based on the calculus in this book, would be: Mexico, Spain, Iran, Turkey, Egypt, Saudi Arabia, India, Pakistan, Indonesia (with virtually inseparable Singapore), South Korea, Brazil, Nigeria, South Africa, and New Zealand, whose strategic fate is inevitably linked with Australia. This list is not necessarily meant to exclude others and some of these will not at present be able or willing to join. India, South Korea, and Nigeria—to name only a few—are in some political disarray at the moment. The list simply indicates that these 15 of the 56 most consequential nations, along with the two lesser powers linked geographically with potential members of the Oceans Alliance, are logical candidates for U.S. guarantees and could be expected to support U.S. strategic aims of the kind recommended.

Such an Oceans Alliance, or new Athenian League, if all of these countries should join, would contain 25 nations possessing nearly 60 percent of the perceived power of the 56 ranking nations (Chapter Seven, page 173) according to my calculus. If these 25 nations were members, the Alliance would have one or more strategic strong points in every politectonic zone except the Soviet and Asian Communist Zones, II and III. In this case it would be more than three times as strong as the leading nations of the Soviet sphere of influence (Zone II) and ten times as strong as Communist Asia. Moreover, the existence of such a powerful Oceans Alliance would tend to lift the spirits and energize the enterprise of people in an area containing the nontotalitarian two-thirds of the world's population.

To guard against hostile inroads into this entire group of 25 would be a clear and reasonable national grand strategy for the United States. If all or most of these nations joined the United States in a system of bilateral but mutually supporting alliances, many of them reaffirming other alliance bonds, the world balance of power would gain enormously in stability. This does not mean the United States would try to preserve a frozen *status quo* in world affairs, which is impossible, but simply that it would work for orderly economic, social, and political evolution without destructive spasms of violence.

Some observers would subtract a few of these nations from a list of major allies; others might add a few.[3] I assume that all of the remaining NATO nations would want to belong and in effect would be brought into an Oceans Alliance through their present treaty relations with the

United States, adding another eight nations, albeit smaller ones.[4] There is nothing final about the selection made above. The basic pattern is sound, however, and if fully understood by U.S. citizens it would provide the nucleus of a national consensus on U.S. strategic purpose and a consequent firming up of national will. The main concept should be that key nations whose interests are compatible with U.S. purposes be included, and that at least one strong nation from each politectonic zone be represented.

Pursuit of detente in the literal sense that has recently come back into use in Washington—in the sense of taking every reasonable step to avoid war and to relax tension over international conflicts—would, of course, continue. The leaders of the United States should, however, disclaim euphoric illusions about this process of the sort that became widespread under the aegis of Nixon in 1972 and 1973. Detente is a condition, not a policy, and tensions will tend to be relaxed if U.S. international purposes are clear and if its strength is adequate for its commitments. Furthermore, American leaders in all informed groups of the society should plainly recognize and explain to the people of this country that crucial short-of-war conflicts over political influence and economic resources in the rimlands of Eurasia or even in the southern hemisphere are likely to continue so long as governments in Moscow and Peking sponsor revolution, class warfare, and guerrilla liberation movements in other nations.

U.S. defense policy and national strategy ought to focus on this danger, not on superficial diplomatic atmospherics. Civility and fair dealing toward all nations are entirely in the U.S. interest. Confrontations would occur only if interventions by totalitarian states occur in areas vital to the security of leading nations in the U.S. alliance system. The United States would continue to try to resolve all conflicts peacefully, but it would not avoid confrontations by making concessions at the expense of its allies or its own interests. This new foreign policy would stabilize international relations and perhaps will permit a realistic *modus vivendi* with the totalitarian nations in due course—though almost certainly not in the immediate future and not until the United States is perceived to have a firm long-term strategy. It would also recommit this country to the political and economic ideals in which most people in the United States believe.

The United States cannot delay long in organizing its own efforts along these lines. Otherwise the trend toward further decline in world perceptions of U.S. power cannot be halted. The remedy lies in adoption of a new strategy, a rebuilding of national will to support it, and a renaissance of energetic alliance-building efforts. Not only would the United States and its allies benefit, but so would those nations low on the scale of present international power rankings whose future fate will be determined largely by the evolution of the balance of power in the 1970s and 1980s. The United States must offer credible security guarantees to its allies in order to prevent totalitarian control of Eurasia. It must also provide imaginative, farsighted economic policies that will bring mutual benefits to the Oceans Alliance nations, tied one to another by the sea-lanes of the world and a sense of common purpose. The United States then can act firmly and honorably to create an international environment safe for the international exchange of economic goods and services, political pluralism, orderly social change, and the nonviolent resolution of conflicts.

Notes

Chapter One

1. The word "tectonic" literally means pertaining to construction or building, or specifically to the structural deformation of the earth's crust, whereby continental plates are gradually shifting relative to one another.

2. We have included for examination in this study 158 states not under foreign jurisdiction.

An exceptional case is the British Colony of Southern Rhodesia. It has been included because it declared its independence from the United Kingdom in 1965 and has been pursuing an independent policy since that time, although never officially recognized by other governments or by the UN. In fact it is at the center of an important international conflict now at a critical stage in Africa.

Of the 158 nations analyzed in this study, 145 are UN members. Technically there are 147 UN members, but two of these are parts of the USSR, Byelorussia and the Ukraine, which were given votes to attract the USSR into the United Nations when it was formed.

Some of today's states are politically fragile; some fragmentation and some merging may occur. As of 1977, however, the 158 nations mentioned in this book represent the commonly perceived independent actors on the international stage.

3. Walter Lippmann, *U.S. Foreign Policy* (London: Hamish Hamilton, 1943), p. 4.

4. A periodic ranking and classification of nations along these lines, giving slightly more severe ratings of some nations than I do, is published annually by Freedom House under the title, "Freedom at Issue." See the January-February 1977 edition, number 39.

5. Walter Lippmann, *op. cit.,* p. 5.

6. A majority vote in the UN can be carried by 70 states representing less than 5 percent of the population of the world and virtually none of the significant power and international responsibility.

Chapter Two

1. All figures on population and territory in this chapter are taken from the *National Basic Intelligence Factbook,* July 1976, DOCEX, Library of Congress, Washington, D.C. They are the latest reliable, mutually comparable, statistics available. Most perceptions of nations' size and population will be based on such statistics, even though there is a substantial time lag in collecting and collating them. Thus perceptions are based on facts that are a year or so out of date, just as our perceptions of the stars come from light which left the stars themselves light years ago. National policy must usually be based on just such perceptions. They are the best evidence available at the time decisions must be made.

2. Note that this multiplies by ten the weights assigned in the 1975 *World Power Assessment.* Since this multiplication by adding one zero is used systematically for all factors in this 1977 assessment, the results are still comparable with the earlier volume.

The employment of index numbers enlarged by a factor of ten simply gives more flexibility and allows more refined judgments in assigning weight values without altering comparative rankings.

3. Raw material economic resources endowment is not included in the discussion of critical mass because it is reflected in the measurement of current economic power in Chapter Three.

Chapter Three

1. *National Basic Intelligence Factbook,* July, 1976, and *Handbook of Economic Statistics 1976,* both from DOCEX, Library of Congress, Washington, D.C. In some cases, primarily in GNP estimates for Communist countries, adjustments and modifications have been introduced to take into account later data or special considerations pointed out in a study prepared by Herbert Block, economic consultant to the Department of State. For his basic methods, see his book published by the Center for Strategic and International Studies (CSIS), Georgetown University, under the title *Political Arithmetic of the World Economies,* 1974. In 1975, the base year of this paper, financial and government interventions produced exchange rates that deviate considerably from true purchasing power parity; the GNPs of the FRG, Sweden, and Mexico are, for example, overstated, while the GNP of the United Kingdom is understated.

2. In 1977 dollars the U.S. GNP will probably be around $1.8 billion.

3. This system of weighting is different from the more simplified method used in the 1975 *World Power Assessment,* which was skewed to the advantage of smaller nations. The 1977 system simply gives every nation a weight equal to two-thirds of the number of tens of billions of GNP, rounded.

4. The energy ratings in this volume are based on more complex data than those used in the 1975 study. For example, negative factors are specifically calculated and oil and coal are separated statistically. The basic approach of bonus values is the same, however, in the two books.

5. *Handbook of Economic Statistics 1976, op. cit.,* and U.S. Department of State, Bureau of Public Affairs, GIST, "Export of Nuclear Technology," October 1976. Statistics also from the Atomic Industrial Forum, Washington, D.C., June 1976

6. The preferred measure is probably the proportion of GNP made up by the manufacture of machines and machine tools. These products especially measure the capacity of the economy to rejuvenate itself (i.e., replace industrial capacity as it wears out) and to expand. Unfortunately, comparative data for this component of manufacturing are not readily available.

Chapter Four

1. Carl von Clausewitz, *On War* (London and Boston: Routledge and Kegan Paul, 1968), Vol. I, pp. 2 and 23.

2. Data for this chapter are taken primarily from Annual Reports by Secretaries of Defense or Chairmen of the Joint Chiefs of Staff. The overall analysis and some details

are based on a special unpublished research report prepared for use in this book by Edward N. Luttwak. It also draws upon Dr. Luttwak's *Strategic Power: Military Capabilities and Political Utility* (Washington, D.C.: CSIS, 1976).

3. *Annual Report, Defense Department, FY 1975,* p. 46.

4. MIRV tests for the SS-N-8 were observed late in 1976.

Chapter Five

1. In comparing this 1977 assessment with the original 1975 volume, readers will note that nuclear capabilities are given weight equivalent to conventional military capabilities. This is simply a change in judgment reflecting the greater plausibility of a threat of use of non-nuclear forces and hence a greater total weight.

2. This methodology, developed in collaboration with Edward N. Luttwak, is much more elaborate but also more realistic than that of our 1975 volume.

3. *The Military Balance 1976-1977* (London: International Institute for Strategic Studies, 1976), p. 104. These numbers are (except for tactical aircraft) the agreed figures in Mutual Force Reduction negotiations which have been going on since October 1973. They include forces stationed in Poland, East Germany, and Czechoslovakia on the Warsaw Pact side, including those of the Soviet Union, and in West Germany and the Benelux countries on the NATO side, including those of the United States. The tactical aircraft figures have been updated from *United States Military Posture for FY 1978* by Chairman of the Joint Chiefs of Staff General George S. Brown, USAF, prepared January 20, 1977, p. 37.

4. *White Paper 1975/1976: The Security of the Federal Republic of Germany and the Development of the Federal Armed Forces,* published by the Federal Minister of Defense, Bonn, 1976, pp. 34-35. References to upgrading of forces taken from *Military Posture, op. cit.,* p. 60.

5. Data used throughout this chapter are taken from *The Military Balance 1976-1977* (London: The International Institute for Strategic Studies, 1976), adjusted in accordance with information in the Annual Reports of the Secretary of Defense and the Posture Statements of the Chairman of the Joint Chiefs of Staff.

6. "Estimated Soviet Defense Spending in Rubles, 1970-1975," Central Intelligence Agency, May 1976, DOCEX, Library of Congress, Washington, D.C.

7. *World Military Expenditures and Arms Transfers 1966-1975,* U.S. Arms Control and Disarmament Agency, Washington, D.C. (New York: Praeger, 1974). For U.S. history, see Murray L. Weidenbaum, *Economics of Peacetime Defense,* p. 25.

8. *World Military Expenditures and Arms Transfers 1966-1975. op. cit.*

Chapter Six

1. In the 1975 *World Power Assessment* this number was 50. The values are thus proportional, if allowance is made for the extra zero (digit), which was added as explained earlier to give a greater range for assigning index numbers and a greater ease in manipulating them. The only conceptual change is in the area of military power,

where nuclear and conventional forces are given a maximum of 100 weights each, instead of 150 versus 50 as in 1975 (then stated as 15 versus 5).

2. *Pravda,* April 5, 1974, commenting on the anniversary of the Soviet-Finnish treaty of 1948, said: "The Soviet-Finnish treaty is confirmed by the whole course of history and, particularly, by the positive changes in the international situation in recent years as a model for the development of relations between states with different social systems. . . . The treaty is an important element of the system of all-European security, whose creation is the common cause of all states on our continent."

Chapter Seven

1. I am deeply indebted to Dr. Russell Jack Smith for undertaking the research and analysis that underlie this whole treatment of national will.

2. Paul R. Brass, *Language, Religion, and Politics in North India* (Cambridge: Cambridge University Press, 1974), p. 15.

3. *Ibid.,* pp. 404-405.

4. Daniel J. Boorstin, *The Americans: The National Experience* (New York: Random House, 1965), p. 427.

5. Jawaharlal Nehru, *The Discovery of India* (Bombay: Asia Publishing House, 1961), p. 60.

6. Gunnar Myrdal, *Asian Drama* (New York: The Twentieth Century Fund, 1968), Vol. I, p. 277.

7. Many of the citations in this chapter are from Foy D. Kohler, et. al., *Soviet Strategy for the Seventies* (Washington, D.C.: Center for Advanced International Studies, University of Miami, 1973).

8. Mao Tse-tung, "On Protracted War," May 1938, quoted in the famous "little red book" entitled *Quotations from Chairman Mao Tse-tung* (Peking: Foreign Language Press, 1966), p. 61.

9. These quotations are from Mao's works found in *Quotations from Chairman Mao Tse-tung, op. cit.*

10. Reprinted in full in Martin Ebon, *Lin Piao* (New York: Stein and Day, 1970), pp. 197-243.

11. If this approach to rating individual nations for national strategy and will seems Olympian or magisterial, the only defense is to point out that it is impractical within the confines of this book to give each country the close political and sociological analysis it deserves. With the invaluable assistance of Dr. Russell Jack Smith we have in this year's assessment developed and followed a specific format in analyzing the national will of the major nations of the world. While this material is too detailed to be reproduced here, the judgments in this book are based on it. Nevertheless the coefficients listed below reflect the author's personal evaluation based on long experience and extensive research in the field of foreign affairs and are only as good as the judgment behind the rating. This is plainly a game that any number can play; if readers disagree with the coefficient assigned, they can substitute their own and adjust the arithmetic or the reasoning reflected in the concluding chapter. If the conceptual framework is valid, all reasonable men and women can write their own conclusions.

12. A distinguished Soviet scholar of international affairs told me privately that my rating in the first *World Power Assessment* was far too high for Soviet national will.

13. For damage done to the National Security Council and the failure to use fully the analytical and estimative capabilities of the Intelligence Community, see an article, "Policy Without Intelligence," by the author of this book, in *Foreign Policy,* Number 17, Winter 1974-1975.

Chapter Eight

1. See p. 30, Chapter One.

2. This core group of 10 varies only slightly from the group of one dozen selected in the first (1975) *World Power Assessment.* The two nations dropped from the 1975 list, the Netherlands and New Zealand, are omitted simply because by this year's calculus they fall below the perceived power level of the rest of the core group. They are of course prime candidates for inclusion in additional echelons of an Oceans Alliance.

3. Reasoned differences of view will arise as to the suitability of choices for the core group of an Oceans Alliance. As with assigning coefficients for national strategy and will, this is a game any number can play. Readers are invited to select their own alliance membership provided they accept the strategic concepts outlined in this book.

4. Greece, Portugal, Denmark, Norway, Iceland, Belgium, the Netherlands, and Luxembourg are the additional NATO members.

Index